# Everybody's Wine Guy

## Guide to Food and Wine Pairing
By Vincent Senatore

Copyright, Everybody's Wine Guy, 2014. All Rights Reserved.

All rights reserved. No part of this publication may be reproduced, distributed, or transmitted in any form or by any means, including photocopying, recording, or other electronic or mechanical methods, without the prior written permission of the publisher, except in the case of brief quotations embodied in critical reviews and certain other noncommercial uses permitted by copyright law. For permission requests, write to the publisher, addressed "Attention: Permissions Coordinator," at the address below.

Everybody's Wine Guy
3930 Galleria Oaks
Texarkana, TX
www.everybodyswineguy.com

# Contents

Prologue ........................................................................................................ 7
Chapter 1 How to Taste ............................................................................ 11
Chapter 2 Preparing Food and Wine ....................................................... 15
Chapter 3 The FOOD................................................................................ 19
    Beef ........................................................................................................ 21
    Chicken .................................................................................................. 24
    Pork ........................................................................................................ 28
    Veal ........................................................................................................ 32
    Lamb or Mutton .................................................................................... 35
    Seafood .................................................................................................. 39
    Cheese .................................................................................................... 43
    Ethnic Foods ......................................................................................... 47
Chapter 4 The Wine or Grape Variety ..................................................... 49
    THE REDS ........................................................................................... 51
        Cabernet Sauvignon ....................................................................... 52
        Merlot ............................................................................................... 55
        Pinot Noir ........................................................................................ 57
        Malbec .............................................................................................. 59
        Syrah/Shiraz .................................................................................... 60
        Petite Sirah ...................................................................................... 60
        Gamay .............................................................................................. 61
        Zinfandel ......................................................................................... 62
        Grenache .......................................................................................... 64
        Tempranillo ..................................................................................... 65
        Nebbiolo .......................................................................................... 67
        Barbera ............................................................................................ 68
        Dolcetto ........................................................................................... 69

Sangiovese .................................................................................. 70

THE WHITES ............................................................................. 72

    Chardonnay .............................................................................. 73

    Pinot Grigio .............................................................................. 74

    Sauvignon Blanc ....................................................................... 75

    Riesling ..................................................................................... 76

    Gewürztraminer ....................................................................... 78

    Viognier .................................................................................... 79

    Sémillon .................................................................................... 81

    Moscato .................................................................................... 82

    Prosecco ................................................................................... 83

Chapter 5 Food and Wine Paring Charts ................................................ 85

    Appetizers ................................................................................ 85

    Beef .......................................................................................... 90

    Chicken .................................................................................... 92

        White Meat Breast .............................................................. 92

        All Chicken Parts ................................................................ 93

    Pork ......................................................................................... 95

    Veal .......................................................................................... 97

    Lamb ....................................................................................... 98

    Seafood ................................................................................... 99

        Crab ..................................................................................... 99

        Clams .................................................................................. 99

        Shrimp .............................................................................. 100

        Scallops ............................................................................ 101

        Oysters ............................................................................. 102

        Lobster ............................................................................. 102

        Fresh Fish .......................................................................... 104

| | |
|---|---|
| Italian | 108 |
| Oriental | 113 |
| Oriental Thai | 115 |
| Authentic Spanish | 116 |
| Mexican/Tex-Mex | 117 |
| Greek | 119 |
| Cheese | 120 |
| Venison | 121 |
| Chapter 6 Glossary of Terms | 122 |
| Epilogue | 124 |

*You "taste" with your nose and not with your mouth.*

# Everybody's Wine Guy's Guide to Food & Wine Pairing

## *Prologue*

My name is Vincent Senatore. I was born in Brooklyn, New York to a couple of second generation Italians. While both of my Italian parents were born in Brooklyn, all of my grandparents and their immediate relatives were right off the boat from Italy and Sicily. After a quick stop at Ellis Island, they were transported to some existing family in Brooklyn and life went on from there. When my mother's mother passed away at a young age, my mother had to quit school at the young age of 14. She needed to become the house mother. Her father, older brother, and sister had to work outside the home and her youngest brother was only six years old. So, at age 14, she was responsible for cooking, cleaning, shopping (daily) for food, and taking care of her younger brother. She was the "Mom."

My mother was a wonderful cook and no matter how bad things were financially, we always had great meals. I never knew how bad things were because the food was so simple and delicious. Give my mother garlic, tomato and olive oil, and she could make cardboard taste great. Needless to say, I grew up in a household that was profoundly Italian with a sense of tradition and family values. At age nine (against my will), we moved to Edison, New Jersey, as did most of our close family. It was a marvelous time with huge family dinners that will always remain as some of my dearest memories. Sunday's main meal usually began at one pm and lasted until we were excused in the very late afternoon. There were always lots of family at these Sunday feasts and the food was always incredible. I really can't remember a single time that I was bored or antsy at the dinner table. The conversation, the stories, and the phenomenal food were mesmerizing to all of us kids and we didn't want it to end. While this was a weekly thing, the holiday meals were an exercise in marathon eating. I can't imagine how we were able to consume that much food. When I relate my experience with Thanksgiving, Christmas, and Easter, I get full just talking about it. We would always begin with fruit cocktail (from a can) and all the kids wanted the lone cherry from each can. Then there was antipasto, soup, pasta, meatballs, sausage, Braciole, and a short recess before the ham and roast beef were served with accompanying side dishes. I can't remember the turkey ever being served before dark. And, let's not forget the Italian pastries and pies followed by nuts and candy. I clearly remember that my clothes fit fine upon the start of the holiday meal. I cannot say the same at the end. But it was the entire experience that lingers in my mind, decades later, when I relate how food became so important to our culture and my heritage.

I tell this story about my family because it says everything about an immigrant family that struggled to live in a new country, and the heritage that was implanted in my genes and my soul. While there were no great chefs or wine experts in the family, this is the basis for my love of food and the art of matching flavors, aromas, tastes, and textures with beverages that will enhance the overall experience in fine dining. I'm not a wine expert or a culinary school graduate. But, my 39 years in the wine industry has given me the experience to see food and wine in a different light. I was lucky enough to be part of some of the best marketing and Sales companies in America. After spending 4 years in Palm Beach, Florida, I landed my first executive position with Seagram's special wine division; Chateau and Estates. C&E had the finest portfolio of French Bordeaux wine in the country. Then I spent a number of years with a company called Vintage Wine Merchants; dealing in 10 of the best properties in California. During the mid to late 80s, California wine was really starting to become a major player in the retail and restaurant arena, and I was right in the middle of it. I absolutely loved that time. However, it was the 90s that brought the real substance to my education and understanding of food and wine. While representing a number of wonderful wineries from Italy and spending countless hours in the vineyards, I really learned how important food and wine were to a culture. Their lives were centered on the afternoon and evening meals. It would be fair to say that I have been extremely fortunate to have experienced some of the finest cuisine the world has to offer, and I thank God that I joined the wine industry, which put the exclamation point next to the word "Gourmet."

## *The Day I Got it.*

"While I celebrate 40 years in the wine industry, it took me 20+ years to really "get it". While I was visiting a winery, in Italy, we broke away for lunch and little did I know that this lunch would change my life . Entering the restaurant, I thought the place was a "dump". (lesson 1; don't judge a book by it's cover) Everyone was drinking wine out of rocks and highball glasses. All plates and platters were different in size and shape. (lesson two: look around, watch the people.) After a few minutes a lady came out and poured us some wine from a pitcher. Finally I settled in and started to realize that this place was packed with people. The food was flowing, Wine glasses were never empty and these people were having a genuinely great time. One hand on the fork, one hand on the glass and animated conversations. I want to hang out with them. This was lunch? I asked our host if this was a special occasion and his answer still rings in my head. "Every meal in Italy is special and should be completely enjoyed as if it were your last." Then it hit me! These people were never putting the glasses or forks down. They would shovel some food in the mouth, start to chew and throw a swig of wine to the already occupied mouth and continued to talk at the same time. Again, I asked about the food and wine in the mouth at the same time. The answer made perfect sense. The wine was like a condiment. It was about the food and wine; made to match perfectly. The wine was from my hosts vineyards and the food was absolutely magnificent. These consumers deliberately tasted every bite there was no separation of the food and beverage. Everybody's Wine Guy is not for the food and wine expert. It's written the average person who wants to enhance the dining experience by learning how to eat utilizing wine as your salt shaker. "

*Chapter 1*
*How to Taste*

First of all, let's get something straight, right now! Contrary to popular belief, we taste with our noses, not with our mouths. There are no olfactory organs in the mouth. The only function of the mouth (taste buds), regarding the tasting of food are: heat, cold, sweet, and tart (acidic). Olfactory receptors or sensory cells in the upper portion of the nose send messages to the brain regarding millions of different odors and smells. Taste buds actually present in the entire palate, tongue and throat. Swallowing, moves air through the throat and nose; creating additional smells and tastes. When we were children and had a bad cold with a terribly stuffed nose, we couldn't smell a single aroma. Even when mom brought the "quintessential healing potion," chicken noodle soup, we really didn't find it all that special. That's because the nose did not get that information to the brain. The stuffy nose blocked the olfactory receptors from doing their job and making the soup taste good. If one held their nose while taking a bite of an onion, there would be absolutely no taste (it might as well have been an apple or a papaya). However, once you open your nose to the air and allow the olfactory receptors to relay the onion smell to the brain...let's just say...you better like the taste of onions. The entire purpose of this book is to get you, the consumer, to open up an entirely new world of flavors and tastes through the addition of wine as a beverage and a condiment.

The glass is another area that could make your experience considerably better. Stemware is not only pleasing to the eye, it's functional. Utilizing the stem to hold your glass will keep the heat from your body away from the ball of the glass where the wine is present. Why; because the body temperature is around 98 Degrees F and your hand will increase the temperature of the wine very quickly. Optimally, we want our red wines to be in our glass at approximately 65-70 degrees and our white wines (depending on the varietal) to be 48- 50 degrees. The heat from your hand could increases the temperature by 5 to 10 degrees every 30 seconds. Serving a wine that is too cold will make the acids contract and give the wine a very sharp bite on the palate. Likewise, serving a wine too warm will make the wine fat and oily. Our goal is to consume our wines at the optimum level of enjoyment. When properly served with food the temperature (of the wine) could be the difference between a huge success or a so, so dinner.

Have you ever tasted a hamburger that was cooked medium to well-done without any of the usual condiments, like ketchup, onion, pickle, cheese, mayo, or mustard? It's not very tasty. A medium to well-done burger will have most of the juices cooked out of it. While most of the fats will be gone, so will most of the "hamburger's" flavor. A well done burger is exceedingly dry. We add condiments to a hamburger to enhance the flavor and present a richer texture. The idea of matching food and wine is certainly not a novel idea. The simple salt and pepper shakers can be found on the table of every American restaurant and "fast food joint" in America. We even offer our condiments in little plastic pouches. The idea of eating a French fried potato, without ketchup, is absurd. Funny thing is, these accompaniments are not available in most European restaurants. The idea of putting ketchup on anything in Europe could cause a major international incident.

Believe it or not, wine is the condiment of choice in most European households. Why? Wine has the ability to enhance the flavors and textures of their local cuisine. Most Europeans shop daily for fresh ingredients to use in their daily meals. Freezers are rare and hardly ever utilized, and the use of preservatives is non-existent. The manner in which a meal is prepared is the way it is consumed. The inclusion of wine at the noon and evening meal is a natural occurrence and is accepted by all. In many households, even the children are given a watered-down version of wine to have with their meals.

This entire book is dedicated to the enhancement of the meal through the introduction of wine. Finding the perfect wine to match the flavors and textures of a specific dish is not as easy as once thought. The old adage, "red wine with meat and white wine with fish" might still be the customary assessment. However, today there are hundreds of variations and flavorings that make your choice a very difficult one. While I agree that a really rich, full bodied Chardonnay can be served with a grilled, baked, or broiled piece of fresh grouper, if the grouper is served blackened, the Chardonnay will be completely overpowered by the black pepper flavors and mouth feel Strangely, wine selection can vary depending on the cut and desired level of cooking. After spending the majority of my career in the California and import wine industry, I have to admit that I really didn't get "it" until food was added to the equation. While my knowledge of the vine was my primary business, the understanding of food has changed my entire perspective toward the word "Gourmet." The first time I tasted (I mean really tasted) the flavors, textures, and aromas of a Maine lobster served with a glass of Pouilly Fuisse, I was literally stunned. I really focused on every piece of butter dipped lobster, while tossing a swig of Pouilly Fuisse in my mouth at the same time. The French style, barrel fermented, barrel aged Chardonnay created a wonderful new flavor that can only be described as "Awesome." It is that revelation that opened my eyes and my palate to the wonderful world of food and wine pairing.

## Chapter 2
## *Preparing Food and Wine*

I'm going to take a wild guess and state that most people will not take a piece of steak from the refrigerator and start eating it (raw, not Tartare!). No, we will remove the wrapping, allow the steak to come up to room temperature, then possibly season the meat with at least salt and pepper or a special rub and marinade. We are preparing to cook the steak. Likewise, we should prepare the wine much in the same way one might prepare the beef.

Likewise, we need to pull the cork and allow the red wine to breathe or release tannins. Tannins are an <u>astringent</u>, bitter plant compound that binds <u>proteins</u> and various other organic compounds including <u>amino acids</u> and <u>alkaloids</u>. Tannins are very important to the preservation and stabilization of red wines. However they're not the best feeling in the mouth. We release the tannins when we open the wine. The air starts the process and we help it along by utilizing an aerator, a decanter or just pouring the wine in our glass and allowing it or aerate on its own.

Never chill your reds below 60 degrees. The cold will contract the acids and make the wine very harsh in the mouth. The whole act of breathing, or aerating, is merely the opportunity to optimize your wine's exposure to air. By allowing wine to breathe, the wine will typically release some of the acids (that allow wine to live for extended periods) and allow the wine's bouquet to open up, give the consumer more taste (remember the nose), and soften the overall mouth feel (sensations felt on the palate, tongue and inside cheeks). Certainly, we want the wine to be served at optimum so we may enjoy the full benefits of the wine's character and its ability to enhance our meal.

As the esters (chemical compounds derived from an acid) are released and offer the nose more aroma, so will the wine taste better. I like to breathe my wine in my glass. Partially because I don't have the patience gene and I really like experiencing the changes while it happens. Further, the glass will offer more surface space for the red wine to aerate and allow those acids and tannins to be freely released. And, the wine will be ready to consume faster. While there are many "experts" that will try to dispel the assets of breathing, there is no doubt in my mind — breathing your reds will enhance the experience.

While we would like to reduce some of the acids that are present in red wine, we really would like to accentuate the acids that are present in white wines. Have you ever been in a restaurant and ordered a glass of white wine and the glass came out frosted or the wine was super cold? The first sip is then usually very sharp to the mouth and gives a slight burn to the esophagus. Then, after a minute or so, you take another sip. This time the wine is not so bitter and smells a bit nicer. Finally, a few more minutes pass by; your next sip is getting pretty good and you marvel at the excellent choice of wine that you made. You might even think that you're getting a bit tipsy. No! The wine is just getting closer to the proper serving temperature and all of those wonderful aromas and smells had been held back by the coldness of the wine. If a wine is too cold, you can't smell it... And, if one can't smell their wine (again, the importance of the nose), they can't taste it either. I recommend that your white be served between 48 and 56F degrees.  At this optimum temperature, the opportunity for the acids to soften and the esters to open up is essential to the tasting experience.

*It's not about the price. It's about the correct wine for the dish. Inexpensive wines can be the best choice if it's the "right" wine.*

*Chapter 3*
*The FOOD*

The following three parts of this book are dedicated to The Food, The Wine, and The Matching. The food portion is a short compilation of some of the major food groups that can be paired with wine. There are many reasons why a red wine goes well with beef. It's not just the color. There are the enzymes, the different proteins, and the methods of preparation (cooking time and seasoning). We will try to offer a logical approach to the reasons why a particular dish matches a specific wine. Then we will offer an area that will be based on the different grape varieties and how the wines will match up to the different food groups.

The last section of this book will offer the ideal match of food and wine. Further, in many cases, the suggested wine might not be available. So we have offered a second and possibly a third selection. I like to use the example of a wonderful dish from Spain: Paella. The ideal wine for a seafood Paella would be an Albariño from the Rioja Region of Spain. However, Albariño may not be available in your favorite wine store or restaurant. While that might be a shame, one could substitute a Fume Blanc or a Sauvignon Blanc that will be a very adequate replacement.

Our goal is to enhance your dining experience. Bringing the correct foods and wines into the equation will offer the consumer a completely new approach to the way you consume beverages and food. Whether you are selecting a wine to match a particular dish or selecting a dish that will enhance a particular wine, this guide will be definitive and easy to utilize.

### Beef

This section is my personal favorite. I love beef in almost all forms and pairing a wine with beef varies with the cut and the degree of preparation or cooking. The natural fats and proteins are a major catalyst in the selection of red wine and the textures and flavors will determine the perfect type of red that will accompany that cut.

Basically, beef is the name utilized to describe meat from cattle. Beef can be produced from cows, bulls, or steers. Certainly, the quality will vary from country to country and the laws governing the growing and harvesting of the meat. Obviously, there is a great deal of control given to the government departments. However, they are in place to protect the consumer.

There are a number of ratings for beef and the prices will vary depending on the cut and the quality of the beef. Here are some of the ratings set by the American market:

**U.S. Prime** – Highest in quality and intramuscular fat, limited supply.

**U.S. Choice** – High quality, widely available in food service industry and retail markets. The difference between Choice and Prime is mostly due to the fat content in the beef. Prime has a higher fat content than Choice.

**U.S. Select** – Lowest grade commonly sold at retail; acceptable quality, but is less juicy and tender due to leanness.

**U.S. Standard** – Lower quality, yet economical, lacking marbling.

**U.S. Commercial** – Low quality, lacking tenderness, produced from older animals.

**U.S. Utility, U.S. Cutter, and U.S. Canner** grade — Primarily used by processors and canners.

There are a number of methods that are utilized in the preparation of Beef.

**Beef can be:**

**Grilled** (barbecued with sauces and rubs; gas, charcoal, and wood smoked)

**Braised** (cooked in a covered container with a bit of liquid in the container)

**Broiled** (heat coming from above the meat)

**Roasted** (hot oven, heat from beneath)

**Fried** (usually in cast iron skillets)

**Stewed** (slow cooked in a water base with flavorings)

Beef can also be cooked to specific levels of doneness. This will be very important regarding the selection of the matching wine:

**Rare** - Cool, red center

**Medium-Rare** - Warm, red center

**Medium** - Hot pink center

**Medium** -Slight pink center

**Well done** - Completely cooked throughout, no pink

Beef is usually the center of attention of any meal and usually commands the plate. This means the surrounding sides or flavors will be secondary. The use of sauces, marinades, and flavoring can alter the tastes and aromas. However, the taste of beef will dominate the plate. Whether you're cutting into a 24 ounce, medium-rare porterhouse or a meatball drenched in red tomato sauce, the wine choice will be determined based on all of the aforementioned cuts, cooking, and flavoring. As you peruse the reference section of this book, you will better understand the reasoning for the wine pairing. With all of that said, remember to really taste that piece of beef. Take a bit more time to chew and take in the flavors and the aromas. Then, deliberately put some of the matching wine in your mouth at the same time that you're chewing and savoring the beef. The third flavor will be an experience that you will not forget.

## Chicken

Selecting wine to match chicken is as varied as the thousands of recipes and preparation techniques. Chicken is a meat that truly blends in with the surrounding flavors. By itself, broiled, baked, fried, barbecued, or rotisserie, chicken has a very specific, simple taste. It is the sauté, batter, sauce, and flavoring that dictate the matching wine.

Chicken is a domesticated fowl that is the most common and widespread domesticated bird in existence. The history of the chicken goes back some 6000 years and the Romans actually began domesticating them over 2000 years ago. The current population of chickens is purported to be over 50 billion. And, there are more chickens in the world than any other species of bird. We farm chickens primarily as a source of food, consuming both their meat and their eggs.

Chickens farmed for meat are called broilers. Chickens farmed for eggs are called egg-laying hens.

The meat of the chicken, also called "chicken," is a type of poultry meat. Because of its relatively low cost, chicken is one of the most used meats in the world. Nearly all parts of the bird can be used for food, and the meat can be cooked in many different ways. Popular chicken dishes include roasted chicken, fried chicken, chicken soup, Buffalo wings, rotisserie chicken, and chicken rice. Chicken is also a major staple of many fast food restaurants. In fact, today there are a number of restaurants that specialize in only chicken (KFC, Canes, and Golden Chick).

Chicken and eggs are very easily paired with wine. Based on the very specific flavors of the different parts of the chicken and eggs, chicken tends to take on the surrounding flavors of the specific dish. Therefore, the matching wine will be more apt to match the surrounding flavors of the dish. An example of this would be: If one produced Chicken Marsala, Chicken Parmigiano, Fried Chicken and BBQ Chicken, and produced all of them utilizing only the chicken breast (white meat), each dish would need a different wine because of the accompanying flavors of each piece of chicken. The Chicken Parmigiano would be best served with a Chianti Classico; Chicken Marsala would be best with Pinot Noir or Merlot; Southern Fried Chicken would be best served with Riesling; and BBQ chicken is best with old vine Zinfandel. If I were just going to have a piece of baked or broiled chicken, without a sauce or flavoring, Chardonnay would be my choice.

Chicken is such a versatile meat, there seems to be no end to the serving possibilities. Further, each ethnic category of chicken preparation will take on the flavors of their region and will require a wine that will meld with the flavors and textures of that country or region. As you peruse the pairing section of this book, notice the wines that have been selected to match with the dish will vary according to the outside flavors of the dish and not the actual flavor of chicken.  The other two members of the fowl family that are consumed on a regular basis is Turkey and Duck.  Turkey is, of course the "star of the show" on America's Thanksgiving Day and can be prepared in a wide selection of different styles and flavors.  Most folks roast their turkey. However, there are lots of people who will deep fry, BBQ, stew, and grill their turkey. And, each production method will require a different type of wine. Further, turkey has two different sections that vary in taste, flavor and texture; white meat and the dark meat. White meat is a bit drier and more apt to blend in with the surrounding accompaniments. Dark meat is juicier, softer and has a unique fowl flavor. Unfortunately, each style will usually require a different wine.  That's why I love Nouveau Beaujolais for the Thanksgiving feast.  The wine is super fruity and works with all of the flavors on the plate.  The other red that goes with turkey is the lighter style Pinot Noir. Duck falls into the dark meat section of our food chart and we will select wines based on the preparation and serving suggestions. Either way, duck loves Pinot Noir.

*Put the Ketchup and mustard away. Use your wine to accentuate the food.*

## Pork

Simply known as the other "White Meat," pork has utilized this slogan to boost its food value and to make more Americans aware of the different qualities and cuts of the meat from a pig. When I think of meat from a pig, the first thing that comes to mind is "bacon." And, I love bacon. Amazingly, the only way to describe the smells and tastes of bacon is "bacon." There are not too many consumables that can boast of their own smell and taste. In fact, bacon is very often used as a flavoring for other food items, like: green beans, shrimp, scallops, filet mignon and on, and on…I have actually used bacon to flavor pork chops! The meat from a pig is also very versatile in the different dishes it offers and in some cases the nutritional value. I just like the taste and I love playing with the seasoning options.

The pig is one of the oldest forms of livestock, having been domesticated as early as 5000 BC. Believed to have been domesticated in the Orient from the wild boar, the nature and diet of this animal allowed people to domesticate it much earlier than many other forms of livestock, such as cattle. Pigs were mostly used for food, but there were many other uses like: their hides for shields and shoes, their bones for tools and weapons, and their bristles for brushes. Pork may be cooked from fresh meat or cured over time. Cured meat products include ham and bacon. Further, pork is particularly common as an ingredient in sausage, salami, hot dogs, and most breakfast sausages. Incredibly, almost all of the pig is utilized in the production of some major food stuff. In fact, the fat of a pig (lard) was one of the most widely used products for frying. Pork is very high in thiamin (vitamin $B_1$) and, with its fat trimmed, pork is leaner than the meat of most domesticated animals, but is high in cholesterol and saturated fat.

The many cuts of pork include:

- Head - The head can be used to make brawn, stocks, and soups. After boiling, the ears can be fried or baked and eaten separately. Nice Chianti?
- Spare rib roast/spare rib joint/blade shoulder/shoulder butt - It can be boned out and rolled up as a roasting joint, or cured as "collar bacon."
- Hand/arm shoulder/arm picnic - This can be cured on the bone to make a ham-like product, or used in sausages.
- Loin - This can be cured to give back bacon or Canadian-style bacon. The loin and belly can be cured together to give a side of bacon. The loin can also be divided up into

roasts (blade loin roasts, centre loin roasts, and sirloin roasts come from the front, centre, or rear of the loin), back ribs (also called baby back ribs, or riblets), pork cutlets, and pork chops. A pork loin crown roast is arranged into a circle, either boneless or with rib bones protruding upward as points in a crown. Pork tenderloin, removed from the loin, should be practically free of fat.

- Fatback - The fat and skin on the back are used to make pork rinds, a variety of cured "meats," and lard.
- Belly/side/side pork - The belly, although a fattier meat, can be used for steaks or diced stir-fry meat. Belly pork may be rolled for roasting or cut for streaky bacon.
- Legs/hams - Although any cut of pork can be cured, only the back leg is entitled to be called a ham. Legs and shoulders, when used fresh, are usually cut bone-in for roasting. Three common cuts of the leg include the rump (upper portion), centre, and shank (lower portion).
- Spare ribs, or spareribs, are taken from the pig's ribs and the meat surrounding the bones. St. Louis–style spareribs have the sternum, cartilage, and skirt meat removed.
- Knuckles, intestines, jowls and all other parts of the pig may also be eaten. Mostly pickled in brine…
- Tail — the tail has a very little meat, but many people enjoy the flavor. It can be roasted or fried, which makes the skin crisp and the bone soft. It has a strong flavor. I think I'll pass on this one.

In my opinion, the greatest asset of pork and ham is the ability to be paired with many different sauces, rubs, condiments, and vegetables. Pork roasts react well with many different forms of seasoning and cooking options.

With all of that said, pairing wine with pork and pork products is as varied as the seasoning and cooking options. Recently, I prepared pork tenderloin by roasting and seasoning it with a simple salt and pepper. The perfect match was a buttery Chardonnay. If I had rubbed it with some Cajun seasoning, marinade it in one of the many available marinades, or barbecued it in a rich sauce, the wine would have been totally different. Like chicken, pork takes on the character of its preparation or accompaniments. Therefore, the wine will be selected around the overall dish and not the meat itself.

Ham is another one of those meats that can be modified with flavoring and accompaniments. Being cured, most hams have a salty side and require wine that blends in with the salt as well as the flavor of the ham. However, most folks will add a glaze or drench the ham with citrus flavors, molasses, and brown sugar. Believe it or not, the best wine with this style of preparation is Beaujolais or a lighter Pinot Noir. Recently, I have found a number of Rose's of Pinot Noir that pair wonderfully with cured ham and work extremely well with most of the side dishes. While it's at its best from November to May, Nouveau Beaujolais is a very exciting match for the very popular Christmas ham, as well as Easter hams and pork roasts.

## Veal

Growing up in the '50s and '60s, veal was a staple in the gourmet side of Italian cuisine. I lived for a Veal Parmesan sandwich smothered on a rich tomato sauce, and fresh Buffalo Mozzarella on a loaf of hard crusted Italian bread. Then there's the Saltimbocca, braised in a rich sauce. Mamma Mia! Surprisingly, veal has been an important ingredient in Italian and French cuisine from ancient times. The veal is often in the form of cutlets, such as the Italian veal cutlets or the famous Austrian dish Wiener Schnitzel. Some classic French veal dishes include fried veal Grenadines (small, thick fillet steaks), stuffed thin sliced veal, and roasted joints. Because veal is lower in fat than many meats, care must be taken in preparation to ensure that it does not become tough. Veal is often coated in preparation for frying or eaten with a sauce. Veal

Parmigiana is a common Italian-American dish made with breaded veal cutlets.

In addition to the very white meat, bones are often used to make a stock that forms the base for sauces and soups such as demi-glace. Most valued are the liver, sweetbreads, and kidneys.

Veal is the meat of young cattle (calves), in contrast to the beef from older cattle. Though veal can be produced from a calf of either sex or any breed, most veal comes from male calves (bull calves) of the dairy cattle breeds.

Matching wine with veal is a bit more difficult than beef because it has its own unique flavor and texture. In some recipes, veal can be very elegant. However, that same elegant cut can be produced in rich sauces and gravies that take the flavors from elegant to robust. Certainly, the wine will be selected based on the flavor and texture of the dish. For example, Osso Bucco, which is usually braised and served in a flavorful sauce, would be best served with an Italian Barolo or a Chateauneuf du Pape. While a grilled veal steak or chop would be best with a Cabernet Sauvignon or Merlot. And the famous Weiner Schnitzel is best with a German Riesling Spatlese.

The many types of veal include:

- **Bob veal**, from calves that are slaughtered when only a few days old (at most one month old).
- **Formula-fed ("milk-fed") veal**, from calves that are raised on a milk formula supplement. The meat color is

ivory or creamy pink, with a firm, fine, and velvety appearance.

- **Non-formula-fed ("grain-fed") veal**, from calves that are raised on grain, hay, or other solid food, in addition to milk. The meat is darker in color, and some additional marbling and fat may be apparent. It is usually marketed as calf, rather than veal.
- **Rose veal** in the UK (generally called *young beef* in Europe), is from calves raised on farms.
- **Pasture-raised veal.**
- **Free-raised veal,** from calves raised in the pasture with unlimited access to their mother's milk and pasture grasses. They are not administered hormones or antibiotics. These conditions replicate those of pasture-raised veal. The meat is a rich pink color. Free-raised veal is typically lower in fat than other veal. Calves are slaughtered at about 24 weeks of age.
- **Special-fed veal** is from calves fed a balanced milk- or soy-based diet, one fortified with 40 essential nutrients, including essential amino acids, carbohydrates, fats, dietary iron, and other dietary minerals and vitamins. As of 2013, the majority of veal calves in the USA are special-fed.

## Lamb or Mutton

I have always wanted to stand on a table in the middle of a castle with a leg of lamb in one hand and a flagon of robust red wine in the other, just like Errol Flynn in those Robin Hood movies (OK, let's leave the tights in the movies only!). He would take a bite out of the meat and a swig from the flagon and fight the Sheriff's men all at the same time. It looked so decadent and delicious. Well, we live in a different time and we now utilize forks and knives. And, we drink our wines out of stemware. But, the food tastes the same and we have a better selection of wine to choose from. The meat from a lamb is unique in flavor and taste and really needs to be properly prepared and cooked. Certainly, the matching wine can be the exclamation point in one of the great feasts of all time.

Lamb is much more valued outside of the US. In countries like New Zealand, Greece, and Spain and throughout the Arabic nations, the meat of the sheep, goat, or lamb is highly prized and a mainstay in their every day dining habits.

Lamb or mutton is the meat taken from domestic sheep species at different ages. A sheep in its first year is called a lamb, and its meat is also called lamb. The meat of an adult sheep is mutton, a term only used for the meat, not the living animals. In America we refer to all sheep-based meat as lamb. The meat of a lamb is taken from the animal when it is between one month and one year old. This meat generally is more tender than that from older sheep and appears more often on tables in some Western countries. Hogget and mutton have a stronger flavor than lamb because they contain a higher concentration of fatty acids, and these are preferred by some. Lamb is often sorted into three kinds of meat: forequarter, loin, and hindquarter. The forequarter includes the neck, shoulder, front legs, and the ribs up to the shoulder blade. The hindquarter includes the rear legs and hip. The loin includes the ribs between the two.

Lamb chops are cut from the rib, loin, and shoulder areas. The rib chops include a rib bone; the loin chops include only a chine bone. Shoulder chops are usually considered inferior to loin chops, and both kinds of chops are usually grilled. Breast of lamb (baby chops) can be cooked in an oven.

Leg of lamb is a whole leg; saddle of lamb is the two loins with the hip. Leg and saddle are usually roasted, though the leg is sometimes boiled.

Lamb shank definitions vary, but generally include:

- Lamb shank is cut from the arm of the shoulder, contains leg bone and part of the round shoulder bone, and is covered by a thin layer of fat and fell (a thin, paper-like covering).
- Lamb shank is a cut of meat from the upper part of the leg.

Thin strips of fatty mutton can be cut into a substitute for bacon.

- Square cut shoulder – shoulder roast, shoulder chops, and arm chops
- Rack – rib chops and riblets, rib roast
- Loin – loin chops or roast
- Leg – sirloin chops, leg roast (leg of lamb)
- Neck
- Breast
- Shanks (fore or hind)
- Flank

In my opinion, Rack of lamb is the most elegant of entrée's when served with grilled or steamed vegetables, mint jelly and red Bordeaux from the Medoc. Leg of lamb and shoulder roasts are best served Mediterranean style, slow-roasted in oodles of herbs and spices. This style of lamb is a bit more oily and moist. But, it is loaded with flavor and requires a robust, round wine like Chateauneuf du Pape or Amarone or a Sonoma Rhone blend.

*Take the time to enjoy every morsel and sip. Look at your meal as a break from the craziness of everyday life.*

## Seafood

Seafood encompasses many different genres of fish, amphibians, and shell fish. If it lives in or around the sea, we tend to categorize it as fish. Most folks categorize seafood into three major groups: mollusks, crustaceans, and fish. I like to get a bit closer to the texture and flavor of particular seafood and categorize it by cooking genre. Shellfish, for example, can be separated by the texture and shell type are known as crustaceans (Lobster, Shrimp, Scallops) and mollusks (Clams, Oysters, Mussels). Crustaceans can be prepared in many different styles. They can be boiled, steamed, baked, grilled, broiled, and sautéed. They all react well to seasoning, sauces and, especially, butter. Further, crustaceans react especially well to big, rich Chardonnays that spend time in oak barrels. The rich texture of crustacean meat and the buttery style Chardonnays are a natural match of culinary excellence. Mollusks, however, are excellent served raw, as well as steamed, broiled, baked, sautéed, battered and deep fried. The flavors of the mollusks are usually salty, high in alkaline, and have a very soft, fleshy texture that is usually consumed with a sauce or a citrus blend. Most oysters and clams, served raw, will also be accompanied with a cocktail sauce, horseradish, and lemon or lime. While the lobster and shrimp work well with Chardonnay, mollusks really need a much different flavor to match the saltiness of the seawater flavor. I really like to match this type of shellfish with a New Zealand style Sauvignon Blanc because of the abundant tropical nose and the clean, crisp finish. In recent times, however, I've found the flavors from a decanted bottle of Prosecco can be an extraordinary match of flavors and textures. The act of decanting a bottle of the Italian sparkling wine, known as Prosecco, will quickly remove some of the bubbles while keeping a fizzy texture that tingles the palate when served with raw mollusks. Decanted Prosecco will also be a great match with fish that have a sharp, iodine finish in the taste (Like Trout or Mackerel).

Fish are aquatic vertebrates which lack limbs with digits, use gills to breathe, and have heads protected by hard bone or cartilage skulls. The main fish groups can be divided into larger predator fish (sharks, tuna, marlin, swordfish, mackerel, salmon) and smaller forage
fish (herring, sardines, sprats, anchovies, menhaden). The

smaller forage fish feed on plankton and can accumulate toxins to a degree. The larger predator fish feed on the forage fish, and accumulate toxins to a much higher degree than the forage fish. So the big fish eat the little fish and the aquatic mammals (whales, dolphins and seals) eat everything. We will concentrate on fish that is readily available in the local supermarkets and seafood restaurants. There used to be a general rule that one would consume white wine with all fish. However, taking into account the preparation and cooking procedures, that rule is a bit more tenuous. For example, one might blacken their fish. A white wine would be completely overpowered by the pepper and the correct wine would be a young California Zinfandel or a lighter style Shiraz. Another cooking style is smoking, BBQ, or cedar plank grilling. The fish picks up specific flavors from the wood, charcoal, or smoke. So, one might utilize a light Pinot Noir, or a fresh Rose of Malbec to accentuate the flavors of the fish. Basically, white wine with fish is a good rule of thumb. Other than the aforementioned flavorings or cooking styles, Chardonnay, Pinot Grigio, Gewurztraminer, Riesling, Viognier, Sauvignon Blanc, Prosecco, and white blends will be the "go to" wines when it comes to fresh fish. Again, we will rely on the cooking style and outside flavoring to determine the proper white wine. Let's use Filet of Sole as our example: If one should bake, broil, or sauté Filet of Sole, I would highly recommend a buttery, rich Chardonnay to accompany this dish. If one cooks the dish exactly the same, but flavors the fish with lemon and fresh herbs, then one might have a Sauvignon Blanc or a Decanted Prosecco as the matching wine. The flavoring (like lemon or a salsa) will dominate the taste of the dish and the usual wines will not blend well. The matching section of this book will offer a number of options regarding the different fish and the wide variety of flavors. However, when in doubt — choose a dry white.

*Focus on the newly developed taste when the wine meets your food in the mouth.*

### Cheese

This is an area that I really enjoy discussing because wine and cheese are such natural companions. However, not all cheeses will match up with all wines and not all wine works with all cheeses.

Cheese is a food produced from milk that is made in a wide range of flavors, textures, and forms. Cheese is comprised of proteins and fat from milk, usually the milk of cows, buffalo, goats, or sheep. During production, the milk is usually acidified, and the enzyme rennet that causes coagulation is added. These solids are separated and pressed into its final type. Some cheeses have molds on the rind or throughout. Further, most cheeses will melt at cooking temperature. That is not always a good thing;

sometimes one wants to keep the solid texture and the fresh nose of a cheese.

There are hundreds of types of cheese that range in flavors and taste based on their country of origin or the regional atmosphere. The many styles, textures, and flavors depend on the origin of the milk (including the animal's diet), pasteurization, butterfat content, bacteria, the mold, processing, and aging. Herbs, spices, or wood smoke may be used as flavoring agents. In some cheeses, the milk is curdled by adding acids such as vinegar or lemon juice. Most cheeses are acidified to a lesser degree by bacteria, which turn milk sugars into lactic acid, and then the addition of rennet completes the curdling.

Cheese is much appreciated for its portability, long life, and high content of fat, protein, calcium, and phosphorus. Also, cheese is more compact and has a longer shelf life than milk so it's easier to keep. Although the length of a cheese's life may depend on the type of cheese, labeling will state that a cheese should be consumed within three to five days of opening. Generally speaking, hard cheeses (Swiss, Manchego) last longer than soft cheeses, such as Camembert or Chevre.

There is some debate as to the best way to store cheese, but some experts say that wrapping it in cheese paper provides optimal results. There are approximately 500 different varieties of cheese that are recognized by the International Dairy Federation. Varieties may be classified into types based on length of aging, texture, production methods, fat content, animal milk, country or region of origin. However, no single method is being universally utilized. Categorizing cheeses by firmness is a common but inexact practice. The main factor that controls cheese hardness is moisture content, which depends largely on the pressure with which it is packed into molds, aging time, and the atmosphere where the cheese is aged. Some cheeses are categorized by the source of the milk used to produce them or by the added fat content of the milk from which they are produced. While most of the world's commercially available cheese is made from cows' milk, many parts of the world also produce cheese from goats and sheep.

<u>Double cream cheeses</u> are soft cheeses of cows' milk enriched with cream so that their fat content is 60% or, 75%. In the case of triple creams, <u>soft-ripened, and blue-vein cheeses,</u> there are at least three main categories of cheese in which the presence of mold is a significant feature: soft ripened cheeses, washed rind cheeses, and blue cheeses. <u>Processed cheeses</u> are made from traditional cheese and emulsifying salts, often with the addition of milk, more salt, preservatives, and food coloring. It is inexpensive, consistent, and melts smoothly. It is sold packaged and either pre-sliced or unsliced, in a number of varieties. It is also available in aerosol cans in some countries.

In any case, cheese will vary in taste, smell or nose, and texture. And, the selection of a wine that will match best is as important as the style of cheese itself. Over the years, I have found that I can utilize the many different Swiss cheeses with almost all wines. However, the harder cheeses, like Manchego and Parmesan, are much better with the tannic red wines because they match well in protein and texture. The softer cheeses, like Brie and Camembert, seem to work better with the white wines. White wines will have a crisper finish and a more flowery nose. Either way, wine and cheese is one of the best matches of food and wine ever created. Add some fruit and hard crusted bread, and you will be duly impressed by the gourmet side of wine and cheese.

*Wine and cheese . . . a match made in Heaven.*

## Ethnic Foods

Selecting wines for an ethnic dish is one of the most difficult tasks any gourmet will face. There are so many different flavors, seasonings, cooking techniques, and serving selections to deal with. For example, there are regional sauces like Italian tomato or French Béarnaise. The taste and smells are completely different and require completely different wines to accompany them. A great example of ethnic cooking is the use of rice. In many cultures, rice is the most important food stuff available to the local consumers. The Spanish utilize many different variations of the rice-based Paella. Italians will use everything from cheese to mushrooms to cook their Risotto. The Greek Spanakorizo utilizes ethnically popular flavors like lemon, olive oil, and spinach to give their famous rice dish its zesty flavor. Oddly enough, I would match this Greek favorite with a bottle of decanted (Italian) Prosecco. It's the only wine that I would consider with the zesty flavor of lemon and the herbal essence of spinach. And, let's not forget how important rice is to oriental cuisine. Most oriental restaurants will serve rice with every dish on their menu.

Each of the different ethnic cuisines will vary in spice and heat. Thai foods and Mexican foods will utilize spicy hot peppers and oils to flavor the main dishes. While German and the Southern USA will lean on batter and deep frying (in lard or vegetable oils) to accentuate their delicious Weiner Schnitzel and Southern Fried Chicken, the Italians and French sauté the same veal and chicken in olive oil and butter. However, both require a different style of matching wine.

While I love making a gourmet meal as authentic as possible, the use of the ethnically matching wine is sometimes difficult. Many of the perfect matches are not available in all markets. Certainly, we would love to have a Greek wine with an authentically prepared Greek dish. However, the proper wine might not be available in your favorite store or in the state where you reside. So, (in the guide) we have tried to offer substitutes whenever possible. There have been many times the perfect wine was not the wine offered in the region of origin. My favorite example is Spaghetti and Meatballs in a red tomato sauce. Many folks like to serve Chianti (possibly in a straw bottle). However, DOCG Chianti is a lighter style wine. If the Chianti Classico or Classico Riserva is not available or too expensive, one might be better off with a soft, rich style Merlot from Sonoma or Central Coast. I have actually found the Merlot to be a much more enjoyable wine with my Spaghetti and Meatballs.

## Chapter 4
## *The Wine or Grape Variety*

When I first began my career in the wine industry, most wines were labeled with the name of a region, winery, brand, or a person's name. In recent times, wines are being identified by the name of the grape variety that is most dominant. Even the great Chateaux of Bordeaux, which are blends of 3 to 5 grape varieties, are now displaying the grapes and the percentage used in their production. There was a time when all red wine was generically called Burgundy and all white was called Chablis. Most Americans did not even realize that Burgundy and Chablis are very important regions in France and the wines generated from those regions are of exceptionally high quality and price.

The astonishing aspect of the Chablis/Burgundy moniker is the wines from Chablis (region) can only be produced from the Chardonnay grape variety and the wines of Burgundy (region) may only be produced from the Chardonnay grape (for whites) and the Pinot Noir grape (for reds). It's remarkable how the times have changed.

Understanding the general components of a particular grape variety will offer the consumer a basic profile of any wine produced from that grape variety. During the 1980s, a number of California brands began a campaign to bring the grape variety to the forefront. From that point on, Americans have taken the lead in the education of the grape. Today, most wineries will provide the consumer the name of the grape or grapes utilized in the production of a particular wine. Additionally, they will offer the percentage of each variety utilized in the making of a blended wine (e.g., Meritage from California). By offering the consumer this information, one can get a fairly good idea of the taste, bouquet, and finish of most available wines. Certainly, it is in the consumer's best interest to have a good understanding of the flavor profile for each variety. So, in an effort to help you better comprehend the different flavors and tastes of each grape variety, the next section of this book is a list of the top grape varieties and their profiles. It is our goal to give you, the consumer, a basic understanding of what you might expect from each variety and what food might be best suited to the selected grape. If you have the menu set, the next section will help you comprehend the type of wine needed for a successful food and wine pairing.

While there are over 1300 varieties of white grapes and 1500 varieties of reds, we are going to focus on the very top varieties that can be easily found within the American market.

## THE REDS

When harvested and brought in to the winery, the juice of the wine is always clear. All red wines get their color, tannins and complexities from the skins which will be in contact with the clear "must" (pre-fermented juice). The maceration time (juice and skin contact time) will determine the style, richness, longevity and ultimate flavor and taste of a particular wine. Based on the tradition of any particular winery, the maceration time can vary from days to weeks. The winemaker will use their judgment regarding the fermentation and maceration based on the vintage, sugar content, acids (PH), and desired outcome.

Today, I believe is a wonderful time for the consumer. Winemakers are vinifing their wines to satisfy the average palate and producing wine that is more accessible to our palate. While these wines will not have longevity, they're at optimum within a short period of time. Certainly, there will always be the masterfully crafted wines of distinction and they will live for many decades. It is a rare treat to be able to consume a wine that has the proper aging and storage. However, the average consumer will drink their wine within

2 days of its purchase and the newer, more accessible wine would be the perfect accompaniment to a fine dish.

## Cabernet Sauvignon

There has been much speculation regarding the origins of Cabernet Sauvignon. Some thought it came from an ancient Roman variety and was cultivated onto the Vinifera rootstock. However, in recent times (1996), it has been proven that it resulted from the offspring of Cabernet franc and Sauvignon Blanc and was most likely a chance match that might have taken place in the 17th century. The origin had never been definitive until 1996.

The classic profile of wine produced with Cabernet Sauvignon tends to be full-bodied wines with high tannins and obvious acidity that contributes to the wine's aging potential. In vineyards that have cooler climates, Cabernet Sauvignon tends to produce wines with blackcurrant (tartness) notes that can be accompanied by hints of green bell pepper and cedar in the nose. In more moderate climates, the blackcurrant notes are often seen with rich cherry and black olive notes, while in very hot climates the current flavors can veer towards the over-ripe and "jammy" side. The style of Cabernet Sauvignon is strongly influenced by the ripeness of the grapes at harvest. When more on the unripe side, the grapes are high in pyrazines and will exhibit pronounced green bell pepper and vegetal flavors. When harvested overripe, the wines can taste jammy and may have aromas of stewed blackcurrants.

Some winemakers choose to harvest their grapes at different ripeness levels in order to incorporate these different elements and potentially add some layer of complexity to the wine.

When Cabernet Sauvignon is young, the wines typically exhibit strong fruit flavors of black cherries and plum. The aroma of blackcurrants is one of the most distinctive and characteristic elements of Cabernet Sauvignon, one that is present in virtually every style of the wine across the globe. Styles from various regions and producers may also have aromas of eucalyptus, mint, and tobacco. As the wines age, they can sometimes develop aromas associated with cedar, cigar boxes, and pencil shavings.

One of the most well-known aspects of Cabernet Sauvignon is its ability to do well in oak, either during fermentation or barrel aging. The softening effect on the grape's naturally high tannins and distinctive wood flavors of vanilla and spice could complement the natural grape flavors of blackcurrant and tobacco. Further, the Cabernet Sauvignon grape variety has the flexibility to blend well with other specific grape varieties, such as Merlot, Malbec, Petite Verdot, and Cabernet Franc (Bordeaux and Meritage blend). The addition of a different grape variety could accentuate and offer a distinctive taste or texture to the wine. The winemaker and master blender are the real stars of any wine making. While the wine is aged in oak barrels, the barrels are somewhat different. So the correct blend of Cabernet and the percentage of other grape varieties will be the real fingerprint of a winery's brand. We, as consumers, rely on that fingerprint to maintain the continuity of a product that we rely on. While our palates are constantly evolving, we are creatures of habit and find enjoyment in specific flavors and tastes.

A great example of a great pairing of wine and food is the Rib Eye steak and specific types of Cabernet Sauvignon. The element that makes Rib Eye steaks is the marble of fats throughout the cut. When grilled, the fats are burned into a buttery flavor and texture. Cabernet Sauvignon is naturally a perfect match to that buttery essence, with its blackcurrant tartness and high tannins. Once you have found the right "Cab" to match your steak and doneness level, you will want that consistency regularly. Cabernet can also be the wrong wine to match a steak.

At optimum, Cabernet Sauvignon pairs best with rare and medium-rare beef. The enzymes and proteins are a wonderful match. Once you cook past medium-rare, the juiciness dissipates, the fats burn off, and the wine will need to be softer and more buttery (like a Merlot).

Beef is not the only food that works with Cabernet Sauvignon. Lamb, veal, and roasted game meats are a wonderful accompaniment to your favorite Cab. Certainly, Cabernet Sauvignon is a wonderful cocktail wine and would be thoroughly enjoyed with stout cheeses and grilled appetizers. Try a personal favorite: Cabernet Sauvignon and Godiva dark chocolates. Now, this is amazing.

## *Merlot*

Merlot is a dark, blue-black colored wine grape grown on the Vitis Vinifera variety root stock. Commonly used as both a blending grape and a single varietal wine, Merlot is one of the biggest selling wines in America. The name Merlot is thought to be the French name for the blackbird, which is referring to the color of the grape. Further, Merlot is well known for its soft texture and jammy mouth fills. Based on its earlier ripening and softer style, Merlot is a popular grape for blending with the harsher, later-ripening Cabernet Sauvignon, which tends to be higher in tannins. Some of the world's finest wines will have some Merlot in the blend. For example, the majority of French Bordeaux are blended with Cabernet Sauvignon, Merlot, Petite Verdot, Malbec, and Cabernet Franc.

A characteristic of the Merlot is the propensity to quickly over ripen once it hits its initial ripeness level, sometimes in a matter of a few days. There are two schools of thought on the right time to harvest Merlot. The wine makers of Château Pétrus, one of the world's finest and most expensive wineries, favor early picking to best maintain the wine's acidity and finesse as well as its potential for aging. Others favor late picking and the added fruit body that comes with a little bit of over-ripeness.

Merlot works especially well as a blending grape and it is widely thought that the Merlot clone is the parent of many other Bordeaux varieties. Further, the Bordeaux blend can now be found in wines that are labeled "Meritage" and offer the consumer a really good quality blend at a value. Certainly, Merlot lends richness to the blend and brings out some of the qualities not found in the other grape varieties. But when produced alone, the Merlot grape variety offers a very distinctive wine with a plum like corpulence to the texture and a mouthful of ripe berries in the taste.

I have found Merlot to be the perfect wine with foods that are drier and short on flavor. I would use the example of medium-well to well done sirloin steak. This piece of beef will have much of the natural juices cooked out of it and will be slightly drier than a medium rare steak. The juiciness of Merlot adds to the overall texture and offers the consumer a wonderful condiment to accentuate the beef flavor. The versatile Merlot can also bring out the flavors of many of our most robust dishes. Stew and crockpot dishes are rich and hearty and Merlot is the perfect wine with to bring that array of flavors together and add balance to the dish.

I like to categorize Merlot in three very different styles: First, the lighter, more fragrant wine with very big flavors that works well with medium-well to well done steaks. Second, the "middle of the road" style that balances the tannins and the fruit. This wine is best with the "Crock Pot" and stew dishes. Lastly, the Merlot that is harvested earlier and slow fermented and aged in wood barrels — this wine will be very high in big, rich tannins and will have great longevity. This is the Chateau Petrus style of wine and would be extremely elegant with great body and a rich, lingering finish. Anyway one wants to perceive it, Merlot is one of the most versatile grape varieties available and offers the consumer very wide latitude when selecting a wine to match a particular dish. One needs only to be cognizant of the different styles before making their selection.

## *Pinot Noir*

Some say the origins of Pinot Noir can be traced back to the first century "CE". This amazing grape is one of the most unpredictable grapes to grow and the resulting wine can vary in style from light bodied to big and rich. The nose will differ from region to region and even from vineyard to vineyard. However, when Pinot Noir is at its best, the resulting wine is truly magnificent. I like to think of Pinot Noir as a velvety mouthful of luscious fruits and aromas reminiscent of black cherries and chocolate. Pinot Noir is always a favorite by itself or served with soft cheeses, and the wine can be at its best when served with a rich entrée. The texture and aroma make some styles of Pinot Noir the perfect accompaniment to a medium rare Prime Rib of beef. Prime Rib has a very distinctive velvety texture that melds with the elegance of a French (Cote D'Or) Burgundy, an estate wine from Oregon or the richness that can be found in Napa's Carneros region. Prime Rib is only one example of an ideal match for Pinot Noir. Certainly, there are hundreds of dishes that would benefit from the aromas and mouth feel of Pinot Noir. For example, one of my favorite dishes is Vodka pasta. I can't imagine any wine that can be better with that than Pinot Noir.

Based on its long history in cultivation, there are hundreds of different clones in vineyards and vine collections worldwide. More than 50 are officially recognized in France alone, compared to only 25 of the much more widely planted Cabernet Sauvignon. The grapes are clustered in the form of pine cones and the vine leaves are rather small. The extremely broad range of bouquets, flavors, textures, and impressions that Pinot Noir can produce sometimes confuses tasters. Traditional red Burgundy is famous for its savory fleshiness, but today's styles, modern winemaking techniques, and new, easier-to-grow clones have favored a lighter, more fruit-prominent, cleaner style (making the wine more accessible to a wider audience.) The wine's color when young is often compared to that of garnet, lighter than that of other red wines, like Merlot. This is entirely accepted and not a liability. Pinot Noir has a lower skin anthocyanin (coloring agent found in the skins) than most other classical red varieties. However, newer styles from California and New Zealand highlight a more powerful wine with forward fruit and a deeper wine that can be similar in color to Petite Sirah in flavor and alcohol.

I have heard some wine people call the grape variety "sexy." I like to take it a step further. I see Pinot Noir as a feminine wine with style and grace. The biggest benefit with Pinot Noir is the many flavors and textures. And, the biggest problem with Pinot Noir is the many different flavors and textures. The consumer needs to find a style that fits their palate and wallet, then latch on to that brand until the palate evolves away from Pinot Noir. Unfortunately, your palate will want a change after prolonged use of any one grape variety or brand of wine.

I really like to try Pinot Noirs from different countries and regions because they have such a wide array of aromas and tastes. For example: Pinot Noir from the Burgundy region of

France will be abundantly fragrant with a rich, velvety mouth feel and a lingering finish of cherries and chocolate. Pinot Noir from Oregon or Northern California will be lighter in color, with higher acids and a long, ripe berry finish. The Pinot Noir from Carneros or Russian River will utilize many of the same Burgundy clones and produce a wine that will resemble the Burgundian style. In any case, the matching food will vary as much as the different styles. From salmon to creamed sauces, Pinot Noir is a wonderful choice as a food match or a delightful cocktail wine. Utilize a local retailer that you trust to keep you informed about the many ongoing facets of Pinot Noir and availabilities.

*Malbec*

Malbec is a deep purple grape variety used in making red wine. The grapes tend to have an inky, dark color and robust tannins and are known as one of the six grapes allowed in the blend of red Bordeaux wine. As a blending grape, Malbec lends substance to the body of a blend and adds deepness of color to the overall product. In recent years, the Malbec of Argentina has made quite a ripple in the wine industry. Argentina's most highly rated Malbec wines originate from Mendoza's high altitude wine regions of Luján de Cuyo and the Uco Valley. These districts are located in the foothills of the Andes between 2,800 to 6,000 feet above sea level. I believe the high altitude allows the grapes to have a longer ripening season that results in richer tannins and a more "jammy" texture. Certainly, when one discusses beef, Argentina ranks among the world's best.

Malbec is naturally a wonderful accompaniment to beef and lamb.

## Syrah/Shiraz

Syrah is a dark-skinned grape variety grown throughout the world and used primarily to produce deep red wine. Syrah should not be confused with Petite Sirah, a totally different style of grape that is smaller and much more intense. The style and flavor profile of wines made from Syrah is highly influenced by the climate where the grapes are grown, with moderate climates which tend to produce medium to full-bodied wines with a spicy style of tannins. Flavors of blackberry and mint, and black pepper notes, can be found in warmer climates like Australia, where Syrah (known as Shiraz) is more consistently full-bodied with softer tannins, richer fruit, and a spicy finish. In many regions the acidity and tannin levels of Syrah (Shiraz) allows the wines greater aging potential and wider food pairing opportunity. Syrah / Shiraz really give the consumer more latitude when pairing spicy foods (Gumbo, Crawfish, and Chili). Shiraz loves spice…

## Petite Sirah

In recent times, this grape variety and style of wine has become very popular among the newer wine consumers and those who are delving into the red varieties. In the 1860s, the French botanist François Durif grew two locally popular grape varieties: Peloursin and Syrah (found as blending grapes in Cote Du Rhone and Chateauneuf du Pape). At some point, the two vines cross pollinated and

Durif discovered a new grape variety. The grape is basically smaller and much more intense. The small berries create a high skin to juice ratio, and produce tannic wines. When the juice goes through an extended maceration period, the extracted color (from the skins) is deep enough to block out the light and stain the glass. Further, when the juice is aged in new oak barrels, the wine can develop an aroma of raspberry and melted chocolate.

California and French Petite Sirah offer the consumer a deep, inky wine that would be better paired with rich cheeses and fruits, rather than a specific entrée. However, I have paired this wine with a Peking duck and Spiral ham with a fruit-filled glaze. I like to consider wine made from Petite Sirah to be fun and interesting. It's a great starter wine for the red wine beginner. However, be prepared to allow ample breathing time. This wine is a very big mouthful.

*Gamay*

Most commonly known as the grape of the Beaujolais, Gamay has won over many consumers because of its super fruity bouquet and finish. The Gamay grape is thought to have appeared first in the village of the Gamay, south of Beaune, in the 1360s. The variety helped growers get back on their feet after the decline of the Black Death. In contrast to the Pinot Noir variety, Gamay will ripen two weeks earlier and was less difficult to cultivate. It also produces a strong, fruitier wine in a much larger abundance.

The French aristocracy found the wines produced from Gamay to be of common quality and beneath their standards. So, in July 1395, the Duke of Burgundy, Philippe the Bold, outlawed the cultivation of the grape throughout the Burgundy Region, due to the variety's occupation of vineyard land that could be used for the more "elegant" Pinot Noir.

Gamay is a very hearty vine which tends not to root very deeply in alkaline soils, resulting in lack of irrigation around the vines throughout the growing season, with an equally high level of acidity in the grapes. Regarding the Nouveau Beaujolais, acidity is softened through carbonic maceration, a process that also allows the vibrant, youthful fruit expressions reminiscent of bright crushed strawberries and raspberries, as well as deep floral notes of lilac and violets. Gamay-based wines are typically light bodied and fruity. Wines meant to be drunk after some modest aging tend to have more body and are produced by whole-berry maceration. The latter are produced mostly in the designated "Cru Beaujolais" areas where the wines typically have the flavor of sour cherries, black pepper, and dried berry, as well as fresh-cut stone and chalk. A Thanksgiving Day staple, Nouveau Beaujolais is the ideal accompaniment to the entire feast. Released with a (worldwide) grand celebration on the third Thursday of November, Nouveau Beaujolais is the first wine released from the new vintage and hits the marketplace just in time for our Holiday dinners. Beaujolais loves ham and other salty foods. And, it can even be slightly chilled.

*Zinfandel*

A great deal of controversy follows the origins of the Zinfandel Grape variety. Many call it America's grape because it was bred here. Some liken the variety to Primativo, a grape that has its origins in the Apulia region, the heel of Italy. Some experts claim the Croatian and Hungarian grape varieties of Crljenak Kaštelanski and Tribidrag to be the parents of Zinfandel. There's also the man who is considered the father of American viticulture and founder of the Sonoma growing region of California, Agaston Haraszthy, who is said to be the creator of the delightful Zinfandel. And, there are some folks that try to connect Zinfandel to ancient grapes that were possibly grown around 6000 BC. All of this is very interesting. However, the versatile Zinfandel grape has created one of the largest and most exciting inroads that I have ever seen. All I know is the grape found its way to the United States in the mid-19th century, where it became known by the name "Zinfandel."

While the Zinfandel grapes typically produce a deep, robust red wine, with a medium amount of acids, the Old Vine Zinfandel is making big waves in the food matching world. One of my favorite food and wine parings is BBQ beef and ribs, drenched in a spicy BBQ sauce and served with a big, rich Old Vine Zinfandel. Old Vine Zinfandels are created from grapes that are grown on vines that are 35 to 75 years old. These old vines only produce a small number of grape clusters per vine and all of the nutrients and complexities are focused toward a few concentrated clusters.

In the United States, a semi-sweet rosé (blush-style) wine called White Zinfandel has six times as many sales as the red wine. This particular style of sweeter wine is produced by cutting the maceration time and slowing fermentation, therefore leaving a pinkish color and residual sugar content.

It's really good with the very spicy crawfish or a shrimp boil. "White Zin" has become one of the largest selling wines in America, where it is basically used as a cocktail. At full ripening, the Zinfandel grape's naturally high sugar content can be fermented into levels of alcohol exceeding 15 percent. Any way that you want to look at Zinfandel, the wines are as diverse as the foods that match them

## Grenache

Grenache, or Garnacha, is one of the most widely planted red wine grape varieties in the world. The grape variety flourishes in hot, dry conditions such as those found in Spain, where the grape probably originated. However, versions of Grenache can be found in the Rhone Valley of France, and in California's central Valley. Wines made from Grenache tend to lack acid, tannin, and color, and are usually blended with other varieties such as Syrah, Carignan, Tempranillo, and Cinsault.

I like to think of Grenache has a light garnet colored with a brown tinge. The wine is usually big and tasty; a delicious wine with a major "kick." Grenache is basically a spicy, berry-flavored wine with a soft mouth feel and relatively high alcohol content. However, the variety needs to be carefully controlled. Pruning keeps the complexities concentrated into a smaller (per vine) yield.

Grenache is the dominant variety in most Southern Rhône wines, especially in Chateauneuf-du-Pape where it can be as much as 75% of the total blend. In Spain, there are varietal wines made of Garnacha and these may be used to make Rosé wines in France and Spain, notably those of the Tavel district in the Côtes du Rhône and those of the Navarra region. Further, the Old Vines version of old Garnacha can be very luscious. Though Grenache is most often encountered in blended wines, varietal examples of Grenache do exist. As a blending grape, Grenache offers body and fruit that it brings without the very tart tannins. Grenache offers the consumer an abundant nose of raspberries and strawberries and a mouth full of round flavors, such as tar, vanilla, and fragrant herbs. This is a wine that would be best served with the rich, herbal roasted leg of lamb or a spicy "Olla" stew.

*Tempranillo*

Tempranillo is a black grape variety widely grown to produce full-bodied red wines in its native Spain. Unique because it ripens earlier by several weeks than most Spanish red grape varieties, the Tempranillo grape variety is the primary grape utilized in the production of the great red wines of Spain's famous Rioja region. Tempranillo has a relatively neutral profile so it is often blended with other varieties, such as Grenache and Carignan, or aged for extended periods in oak where the wine easily takes on the flavor of the barrel. Tempranillo is an early ripening variety that tends to thrive in chalky vineyard soils such as those of the Ribera del Duero region of Spain.

During the 1990s, Tempranillo started experiencing a revitalization in worldwide wine recognition. This surge began partly as a result of the efforts of a "new wave" of Spanish growers who showed that it was possible to produce wines of great character and quality in areas outside of the Rioja region. One result of this has been that Tempranillo varietal wines have become more common, especially in the better-suited, cooler Spanish regions like Ribera Del Duero, Navarra, and Penedès. Spanish wines are often labeled according to the amount of aging the wine has received. When the label says vino joven ("young wine") or "sin Crianza," the wines will have undergone very little, if any, wood aging. Depending on the producer, some of these wines will be meant to be consumed very young — often within a year of their release. Others will benefit from some time aging in the bottle. For a vintage year to appear on the label, a minimum of 85% of the grapes must be from that year's harvest. The three most common aging designations on Spanish wine labels are Crianza, Reserva, and Gran Reserva. Look for these designations and enjoy them with Paella and roast lamb.

Crianza red wines are aged for two years with at least six months in oak. Crianza whites and rosés must be aged for at least one year with at least six months in oak.

Reserva red wines are aged for at least three years with at least one year in oak. Reserva whites and rosés must be aged for at least two years with at least six months in oak.

Gran Reserva wines typically appear in above average vintages with the red wines requiring at least five years aging, 18 months of which in oak and a minimum of 36 months in the bottle.

*Nebbiolo*

The primary grape of the "King of Italian Wines": Barolo. It is primarily found in the Piedmont region of Italy. The Piedmont region is considered the best home for Nebbiolo and it is where the grape's most notable wines are made. The two most well-known Nebbiolo wines are the DOCG (Denominazione di Origine Controllata e' Garantita governing body of the Italian wine industry controlling planting and production) wines of the Barolo & Barbaresco zones near Alba. Barbaresco is considered the lighter of the two and has less strict DOCG regulations, with the normal bottlings requiring only nine months in oak and 21 months of total aging and the Riserva bottlings requiring 45 total months of aging. In contrast, the Barolo DOCG requires one year in oak and three years total aging for normal bottlings and 57 months total aging for Riserva. The minimum alcohol levels for the two regions vary slightly, with Barbaresco requiring a minimum of 12.5% and Barolo 13%. Wines made from Nebbiolo are characterized by their abundant acids and tannins. Most examples are wines built for aging and some of the highest quality vintages need significant age before they are at optimum. Many of these wines have the ability to improve in the bottle for upward of 30 years. As Nebbiolo ages, the bouquet becomes more complex and tempting, with aromas of tar and roses being the two most common notes. Other aromas associated with Nebbiolo include dried fruit, leather, licorice, and spice as well as fresh herbs. While Barolo and Barbaresco tend to be the heaviest and most in need of aging, wines made in the modern style are becoming more approachable at a young age. The lighter, less tannic styles from Carema, Langhe, and Gattinara tend to be ready to drink within a few years of vintage and are considerably less expensive. While these great wines are really wonderful with roasted meats and cheeses, I like to just enjoy the essence of the wine without any outside flavors. Just the glass and the wine…

## Barbera

Barbera is another grape variety that can be found in the Piedmont region of Italy and is now widely planted in many other grape growing regions. Barbera is a red Italian wine grape variety that, as of the year 2000, was the third most-planted red grape variety in Italy. It produces good yields and is known for deep color, low tannins, and high levels of acid. When young, the wines offer a very intense aroma of fresh red- and blackberries. In the lighter versions, one might find hints of cherries and raspberries, and with more full bodied version, one might find scents of blackberry and black cherries. Many producers will use toasted oak barrels, which provides for increased complexity, aging potential, and hints of vanilla notes. Often the addition of oak aging will complement the high alcohol content and make the new wine more capable of cellaring.

The wines of Barbera d'Asti tend to be bright in color and elegant while Barbera d'Alba tends to be deeper color with more intense, powerful fruit. In the Alba region, many of the best vineyard sites are dedicated to Nebbiolo, with Barbera relegated to secondary location, which limits the quality and quantities of the wines labeled with the Barbera d'Alba DOC. In California, Barbera is the most successful of the

Piedmontese grapes to be grown in the state. In recent years, the fashion of Italian grapes has caused more California winemakers to look into producing high quality varietal Barbera. Barbera growers in the cooler regions of Napa and Sonoma have produced some successful examples, and Washington State producers have been experimenting with plantings of Barbera in the Red Mountain, Walla Walla, and Columbia Valley. Try this wine with Tagliatelle (pasta) in a mushroom sauce with bits of white truffles from the Piedmont region of Italy.

## *Dolcetto*

Dolcetto is a deep black-colored Italian wine grape variety widely grown in the Piedmont region of northwest Italy. The Italian word Dolcetto means "little sweet one," but it is not certain that the name originally carried any reference to the grape's sugar levels. In any case, the wines produced are nearly always dry. Dolcetto can be very tannic and rich with a fruity essence and a moderate to low level of acidity. Dolcetto is meant to be consumed young — typically, one to two years after release. Dolcetto wines are known for hints of black cherry and licorice with some prune-like flavors. While the name implies sweetness, the wines are usually very dry. The dark purple skin of Dolcetto grapes have high amounts of anthocyanin, which require only a short maceration time with the juice to produce a dark-colored wine. The amount of skin contact will clearly affect the resulting tannins in the wine. I prefer this delicious red with Ragu style tomato-based pasta sauces and pizza. I like to think of this wine as the Italian Petite Sirah. The wine benefits from the taste of hard, sharp cheeses like Asiago or Reggiano.

## Sangiovese

One of the most famous grape varieties that nobody really knows about, Sangiovese is a red Italian wine grape variety commonly known as the primary grape of Chianti. While not as aromatic as other red wine varieties such as Pinot Noir, Cabernet Sauvignon, and Syrah, Sangiovese often has a flavor profile of sour red cherries with earthy aromas and tea leaf notes. Wines made from Sangiovese usually have medium-plus tannins and high acidity, which is great with pizza. When aged in wood barrels and in the bottle, the wines tend to become richer and more elegant. Wines from the historical center of Chianti are called Chianti Classico and there are a number of Consortiums or trade groups that have been producing Chianti Classico since the 1400s. The governing body over Chianti is known as the DOCG (Denominazione di Origine Controllata e' Garantita) controls the production all Chianti products. For example, the DOCG will determine the number of vines that can be planted, plant spacing, pruning, size of the crop, alcohol levels, and the legal amount of wine that can be produced from each vineyard. Further, the DOCG issues stamps that are affixed to the neck of the bottle that will guarantee the wine is legal and from the designated vineyard growing area. Some of the higher level clones of Sangiovese are Brunello (Sangiovese Grosso) and Prunotto (famous for Vino Nobile di Montepulciano). These super-wines are always considered the top of Italy's production and command world class attention. Sangiovese is also widely planted throughout Italy and is starting to develop a following from regions like Sicily, Marche, and Apulia. Further, these wines are somewhat richer and softer — perfect for those spaghetti and meatball nights.

*Listen to your brain telling you about the flavors and the tastes. Sip, don't guzzle!*

## THE WHITES

Unlike red wines, white wine can be made from white grapes and red grapes. Just separate the skins from the juice before fermentation, and the result is white wine. During fermentation, white musts will react to the temperature and the vessel that it ferments in. There are many white that are well suited to oak barrel fermentation as well as, steel or glass lined tanks. Obviously, the barrel fermented wines will give the wine a woody or smoky nose and flavor. Cold fermentation will take longer. But the wine will maintain the fruity character. Higher temperatures will make the process go considerably faster; leaving out some of the complexities. Serving your whites will require a bit of chilling. One should be careful not to chill their whites too much. Making the wine too cold will condense the natural acids and make them bit the palate and throat. As the wine comes up in temperature, the roundness and flavors will come forward. Have you ever ordered a glass of white wine from a restaurant and is so cold that is causes condensation on the outside of the glass? Then you take your first sip and the acids draw your cheeks together. Then, you take the next sip and it's a litter better and the next sip is even better. Well, you are not getting intoxicated… The wine is just coming up to the proper temperature and the acids are softening. Try chilling your wine in ice water. This will get you to the proper temperature in a very quick time and keep the wine perfectly chilled in the bucket.

*Chardonnay*

The Chardonnay grape owes its existence to the Romans (in the 1st century "CE"), who first planted the grape known a Gouais Blanc and Pinot Blanc from plants that they brought with them from Croatia. Through generations of cultivation and cross breeding, Chardonnay has become the dynamic white variety that I like to think is the ideal food wine. The versatile Chardonnay grape can be fermented in steel or oak and aged in the same barrels or tanks that it was fermented in. Further, by inoculating the new wine with a type of bacteria, the process known as Malolactic fermentation will convert malic acid (found in apples) to lactic acid that is rich and buttery. Chardonnay can be served with a myriad of dishes, ranging from fresh seafood to rich cream sauces over veal or pork. And, if that's not enough, the Chardonnay grape is a major contributor to the production of Champagne and sparkling wine.

The term Blanc de Blanc infers that the wine was produced from 100% Chardonnay. And Chardonnay is the only white grape permitted to grow in Burgundy and Chablis. The great and very expensive Montrachet, Musigny, and Corton Charlemagne may only be produced from Chardonnay grown within the borders of the Burgundy region. These magnificent white wines have been known to sell for $200-$500 per bottle and are very rare. I look at Chardonnay from a different perspective.

I love the rich, buttery texture and the scent of toasted oak with the rich mouthful of full-bodied wine with a finish of green apple and pineapples. But, I'm not all that willing to spend the necessary big dollars for the aforementioned wine. So, there are many different styles of Chardonnay. While many experts feel the Chardonnay wines are not great with food, I will argue that there is no better wine with shellfish, lobster, crab, shrimp, and freshly caught lake fish.

The real issue is bringing the different styles into perspective and pairing them up with the proper food. I do love the big, buttery style. But, it's not necessarily the ideal wine for a particular dish. If Chardonnay is fermented in steel tanks and aged in steel, the wine will be crisp and clean with a higher acid base. This is a great wine to match with salads, tuna, salmon, and fruit trays; it is also excellent as a cocktail wine and great with soft cheeses. Chardonnay that is fermented and aged in oak barrels and goes through malolactic fermentation will be big and buttery with a hint of apple in the nose and soft acids. This style is suited for shrimp and lobster. Use the attached guide to match the wine with appropriate food. The guide will offer a style of Chardonnay.

### Pinot Grigio

Native to northeastern Italy, the Pinot Grigio grape took America by storm during the early 1990s. California wines were suffering through a tough time with phylloxera, and the prices of California wine were high. And Pinot Grigio was just getting America's attention. Italy's most popular white wine, Pinot Grigio is a major part of Italy's northeast region of Alto Adige, Veneto, and Friuli. The wine is typically fermented dry with an abundant nose of fresh cut fall flowers and light, crisp, mouthful tangy acidity.

Pinot Grigio is usually fresh and fruit-filled, with a relatively short shelf life. As for color, Pinot Grigio is typically a pale, straw-like yellow with some golden hues thrown in. It has a very smooth, satin texture that leaves a pleasant taste on the palate but finishes clean and crisp. Pinot Grigio from Italy tends towards a lighter body style. However, the same grape in France, Germany, and America are a bit fuller-bodied than the Italian style and tend to have a lasting finish of stone fruit and pineapple.

Pinot Grigio can be an excellent accompaniment to many dishes and our guide will offer quite a few matching opportunities. The best part of consuming Pinot Grigio is that it makes a great cocktail wine that matches up with antipasto and rich, flavorful cheeses.

*Sauvignon Blanc*

In recent years, Sauvignon Blanc has bludgeoned in notoriety and new styles. The Sauvignon Blanc grape traces its origins to western France in the Loire Valley and Bordeaux Regions. While it is not clear that the vine originated in western France, experts suggest that it may have come from the Savagnin variety. At some point in the 18th century, the vine paired with Cabernet Franc and formed the famous Cabernet Sauvignon grape variety.

The migration of Sauvignon Blanc has been an immense success for the variety finding homes in every major grape growing region in the world. The southern hemisphere has been especially good to the grape with the spectacular wines from New Zealand. In contrast to the full bodied, acidic Sauvignon Blanc of France and Northern California, New Zealand Sauvignon Blanc offers a nose full of tropical fruit highlighted with grapefruit and pineapple, a clean fresh mouth of tingly acids, and a crisp, short finish. There is no better wine with herbal dishes like pesto and green salads.

In contrast to the New Zealand style, wood aging imparts smokiness and a deeper flavor. These wines are usually richer in the mouth and have a lengthy finish. Then there is the unoaked Sauvignon Blanc with a clean, grassy (fresh cut lawn) essence and a super dry mouth feel. These wines are great cocktail wines and react wonderfully with sea fishes like Swordfish and Ahi Tuna. The attached guide will list a myriad of food matching opportunities for Sauvignon Blanc, utilizing the many different facets of the variety.

## Riesling

Riesling is a white grape variety which originated in the Rhine region of Germany. It is an aromatic grape displaying flowery, almost perfumed, aromas as well as high acidity. It is used to make dry, semi-sweet, sweet, and sparkling white wines. Riesling wines are usually not aged in barrels and offer the consumer a very unique mouth full of wine. As of 2004, Riesling was estimated to be the world's 20th most grown variety and it is usually included in the "top three" white wine varieties together with Chardonnay and Sauvignon Blanc.

Riesling is a variety which is highly sensitive to the soil and climate and the character of Riesling wines is clearly influenced by the wine's regional differences. Higher altitudes and rockier soils have been the best environments to foe growing Riesling; which needs the longer time on the vine. Washington State, Oregon, and California are prime Riesling vineyard areas and produce a very crisp, high acid wine with a wonderful mouthful created by the subtle sugars. The most expensive wines made from Riesling are late harvest dessert wines, produced by letting the grapes hang on the vines well past normal picking time.

There are a number of stages in which German Rieslings are offered. The lightest and the crispest are the Tafelwein and OBA wines. These grapes are harvested at the initial picking time and have the least amount of residual sugar. There will be clusters that will be a bit more ripe and they will be vinified as "Kabinett." This is a bit fuller style but still fresh and clean. A couple of weeks later, the second picking will occur and these wines will be labeled "Spatlese" (late harvest). At the same time, selected grape clusters will be riper and they will be set aside to create "Auslese" (selected picking). Spatlese and Auslese will be considerably sweeter and have a richer texture. Sometime later, after the Spatlese is in the tank, Beerenauslese and Trockenbeerenauslese will be collected through evaporation caused by the fungus Botrytis Cinerea ("noble rot") or by freezing, as in the case of ice wine (Eiswein). Water is removed and the resulting wine offers richer layers on the palate.

These concentrated wines have infinitely more sugar, more acid, concentrated flavor, and deeper complexity. Usually these Predikat wines are served with dessert or on their own with unique fruits and nuts. Riesling can be served with a wonderful array of different foods. I love telling folks that the perfect wine with their fried chicken or catfish is a crisp Riesling. The slight residual sugar matches extremely well with the oils and fats utilized in the fried food production. There are lots of great pairings for the different styles of Riesling in the guide.

## Gewürztraminer

Gewürztraminer is an aromatic wine grape variety, with a hint of spice that is utilized in white wines, and which grows best in cooler climates. As a grape variety, Gewürztraminer has a pinkish red skin color, which confuses the average person because the wine itself is white. Gewürztraminer has high natural sugar and the wines are light straw colored and usually off-dry, with a flamboyant bouquet of lychees and honey. Oddly enough, Gewürztraminer and lychees share the same aromas and aftertaste. Dryer Gewürztraminers may also have aromas of roses, passion fruit, and floral notes. It is somewhat noticeable that many of the different styles of Gewürztraminer have a bit of a Frizzante or the feeling of tiny bubbles on the tongue and palate.

Since we taste with our noses, Gewürztraminer confuses the palate by offering a unique flavor to a very abundant bouquet. That is why, in my opinion, there is no better wine with Oriental food than Gewürztraminer — especially for Thai and Hunan food. The sweetness and fragrant nose may offset the myriad of spices found in Asian cuisine.

Gewürztraminer, like Riesling is great with fried foods with spicy breading. I love Gewürztraminer with Tex Mex cuisine as well. There are not too many wines that can stand up to jalapeño or habanera peppers. The wine really shows best with any spicy sauce or unusual spices.

The French Alsatian style of Gewürztraminer offers a bigger mouthful of rich flavor that really stands up to the hot spices. Northern California and Washington State offer a leaner style of Gewürztraminer with a crisp, clean finish. This style really works well with soft, fragrant cheeses, Tamales, Tacos, and deep-fried Jalapeño poppers. Let me further say that Gewürztraminer makes a great afternoon, poolside wine that can be served cold and without a food accompaniment. It's a really fun wine…

## *Viognier*

Viognier is another white wine grape variety that offers the consumer a big mouthful of wine and matches well with spicy Asian cuisine. Viognier is the only grape variety permitted in the production of the French wine Condrieu, in the Rhône Valley. Mostly the grape is used as a blending grape and is part other Cote du Rhone and Chateauneuf du Pape wines. Outside of the Rhône, Viognier can be found in regions of North and South America as well as Australia and New Zealand.

Like Chardonnay, Viognier has the potential to produce full-bodied wines with a lush, soft character. In contrast to Chardonnay, the Viognier varietal has more aromatics that include notes of peach, pears, violets, and minerals. For some, the initial bouquet of Viognier is a bit hard to palate.

However, with a bit of aeration in the glass, the wine opens up and becomes much more accessible.

The potential quality of Viognier is also highly dependent on vineyard practices and regional climate. Viognier needs a long, warm growing season in order to fully ripen. However, if you have a climate that is too hot, the grape develops high levels of sugars, and the alcohol will stop fermentation before its aromatic notes can develop.

Viognier is naturally a low yielding variety which can make it financially difficult to grow in some vineyards. Many California wineries began experimentation with the grape, only to find it too expensive to maintain. Viognier wines are well known for their rich, floral aromas and terpenes (astringency), which are also found in some Muscat and Riesling wines. Aging these wines will often yield a very crisp drinking wine which is almost completely flat in the nose. The color and the aroma of the wine suggest a sweet wine but Viognier wines are predominantly dry. It is a grape with low acidity; it is sometimes used in a blend to soften wines made predominantly with the red Syrah grape.

Depending on the winemaking style Viognier can often hit its peak at one year of age, though some can stay at high levels of quality for up to ten years. Typically, Condrieu wines are the Viognier style most often meant to be drunk young, while Californian and Australian wines can handle age a little bit better. I am a big fan of the Australian style of Viognier because it offers a drier alternative to Gewurztraminer and Riesling when consumed with spicy foods.

## *Sémillon*

Sémillon is a golden-skinned grape used to make dry and sweet white wines, mostly in France and Australia. The grape ripens early when grown in warmer climates. The Sémillon grape has a low acidity and an almost oily texture. It has a high yield and wines based on it can age a long time. Along with Sauvignon Blanc and Muscadelle, Sémillon is one of only three approved white wine varieties in the Bordeaux region. The grape is also the key to the production of sweet wines such as Sauternes and Barsac. In France, the Sémillon grape is grown mostly in Bordeaux where it is blended with Sauvignon Blanc and Muscadelle. When dry, it is referred to as Bordeaux Blanc and is permitted to be made in the appellations of Pessac-Léognan, Graves, Entre-Deux-Mers and other less-renowned regions. However, when used to make the sweet white wines of Bordeaux (such as those from Sauternes, and Barsac), it is often the dominant variety. In such wines, the vine is exposed to the "noble rot" of *Botrytis Cinerea*, which consumes the water content of the fruit, concentrating the sugar present in its pulp. When attacked by Botrytis Cinerea, the grapes shrivel (raisin-like) and the acid and sugar levels are pronounced.

Obviously, the wines of Sauternes and Barsac are very expensive, but they are well worth the cost. The most famous of these is Chateau d'Yquem. In many vintages, Chateau d'Yquem could cost as much as $500 per bottle. Some of the older vintages (like the 97 vintage) could be closer to $1000. Not to fret. There are many other wines from Sauternes and Barsac that can be found for considerably less, such as $20 to $50. Based on the nature of the wine, it's definitely a dessert wine. But I would never share my palate with food when tasting a bottle of Sauternes or Barsac. It's way too good for dessert...

## Moscato

Today, Moscato is the hottest wine varietal in America. The odd thing about this is the grape has an ancient history and the wines have been available in America since the repeal of Prohibition. Among the most notable members of the Muscat family are Muscat blanc à Petits Grains, which is the main grape variety used in the production of the Italian sparkling wine, Asti (also known as Moscato Asti), made in the Piedmont region.

Mainly known today as Asti, this sweet luscious grape variety is rich in aromatic tones of vanilla and fresh pears. The mouth is completely enveloped in luscious textures and the finish lingers with a tasty blend of citrus and peach. While Italy has had the franchise in Moscato for many years with Asti Spumante, today all of the major wine growing regions have jumped on the "Bandwagon." The wine is available in three major styles. The still wine (no bubbles) offers the consumer a really rich mouth fill of rich, oily-like flavor with a lasting finish. The new and exciting style is the slight fizz or Frizzante style with about a third of the PSI (bubbles) of a full sparkling wine. This style is very refreshing and works really well with a tray of fresh melon, strawberries, and peaches. It's a wonderful "poolside" wine. Then there's the full blown sparkling sensation: Asti. A wine designated DOCG by the Italian Government, this wine is the perfect "toast" wine, as well as the ideal wine with your favorite birthday or wedding cake. What a great way to celebrate a momentous occasion.

## *Prosecco*

I have offered many different food and wine pairings in the guide section of this book and you will see the term "Decanted Prosecco" when searching for a wine that matches up to antipasto, baked fish, and a number of other dishes with hints of lemon and capers. One of the most unique aspects of food and wine matching is finding the perfect match, and Prosecco has given us an exciting new entry to the perfect match with specific food.

Prosecco is an Italian white sparkling wine, generally dry or extra dry. It is made from Glera grapes, formerly known also as Prosecco. The name is derived from the Italian village of Prosecco near Trieste, where the grape may have originated. DOC Prosecco is produced in the regions of Veneto and Friuli, with the best vineyards in the areas of Conegliano and Valdobbiadene (now designated DOCG) in the hills north of Treviso. Prosecco is the ultra famous main ingredient of the Bellini cocktail and can be a considerably less expensive substitute for French Champagne.

Prosecco usually is produced using the Charmat method, where the secondary fermentation takes place in stainless steel tanks rather than the bottle, making the wine less expensive to produce. The rules for the DOCG Prosecco Valdobbiadene are now allowing the use of the Méthode Classico: secondary fermentation in the bottle.

So, why is Prosecco so wonderful, besides the price? The wine has a wonderful, fresh cut floral nose, a bone dry mouth, and a delicious clean, crisp finish. Prosecco is almost confusing to the palate because the wine is so fragrant and so dry and crisp. Further, when this sparkler is decanted, it opens up the floral nose and enriches the flavors. I've never found a wine that works so well with lemon, salad dressings, and brine from pickles, artichoke hearts, and capers. Further, Prosecco is a wonderful mixer with orange juice for Mimosas, Peach nectar for Bellini's, and Cassis for the delicious Kir Royale. With all of that said, I'm really hooked on the sparkling wine for any celebration that calls for a glass of very refreshing, sparkling wine.

*Remember ... serve your wine at the proper temperature!*

# Chapter 5
## *Food and Wine Paring Charts*

PLEASE NOTE: I have provided alternative selections to use when the preferred wine is not available.

## Appetizers

| Food Selection | Wine | Alternative Wine Selection |
|---|---|---|
| Fried Mushrooms W/Horseradish Sauce | Rose' of Pinot Noir | |
| Shrimp Cocktail | Chardonnay big, woody, buttery | |
| Fruit Salad | Chardonnay big, woody, buttery | Prosecco |
| Pupu Platter W/Asian Dipping Sauce | Gewurztraminer, Late harvest Riesling | |
| Queso W/ Tortilla Chips | Garnacha or Grenache | |
| Antipasto | Decanted Prosecco, Pinot Grigio, | Prosecco, Fume Blanc |
| Hummus | Beaujolais | Rose of Malbec |
| Eggplant Salas | Viognier | New Zealand Sauvignon Blanc |
| Jalapeno Poppers | Gewurztraminer | |
| Blooming Onion | German Spatlese | Rose of Pinot Noir |

| | | |
|---|---|---|
| Beer Cheese | Merlot, Merlot Blend | |
| Salmon Tartare | Light style Pinot Noir | Rose of Malbec |
| Seven Layer Dip | Gamay/ Beaujolais | |
| Shrimp Toast | Chardonnay (big and wood aged) | |
| Buffalo Wings/ BBQ, Hot And Spicy, Teriyaki | Old Vine Zinfandel Petite Sirah | Shiraz |
| Chicken Fingers | Riesling or Gewurztraminer | |
| Tapas Plates W/ Olives, Pita, Oils And Salami | Tempranillo, Crianza | Chianti DOCG |
| Spring Roll Asian Sweet And Sour Sauce | Old Vine Zinfandel | |
| Crab Puff | Chardonnay (unoaked) | |
| Toasted Ravioli W/ Marinara Dipping Sauce | Chianti Classico, | Central CA Merlot |
| Mozzarella Sticks /Marinara Sauce | Chianti DOC, | Merlot |
| Chili Con Queso | Garnacha or Petite Sirah | |
| Crab Ragoon | Dry style Riesling | Unoaked Chardonnay |

|  |  |  |
|---|---|---|
| Crustino | See Bruschetta |  |
| Onion Rings | German Riesling |  |
| Egg Drop Soup | Chardonnay (full bodied, and buttery) |  |
| Potato Wedges Or Skins | Rose of Pinot Noir | Viognier |
| Oysters, Clams, Raw | Chardonnay (slight oak aging or un-oaked) | Fume Blanc, Sancerre |
| Oysters, Clams, Stuffed | Tavel Rose | Rose of Malbec |
| Tostada | Grenache |  |
| Guacamole | New Zealand Sauvignon Blanc |  |
| Artichoke Dip | New Zealand Sauvignon Blanc |  |
| Italian Meatballs | Barbera d'Asti, Sangiovese Toscana |  |
| Lettuce Wraps | Sauvignon Blanc |  |
| Shrimp Puff Balls | Sauvignon Blanc |  |
| Spinach Pinwheels W/ Ham | Nouveau Beaujolais |  |
| Spinach Balls | Pinot Grigio |  |
| Bacon Wrapped | Alsatian |  |

| | | |
|---|---|---|
| Jalapeno | Gewürztraminer | |
| Garlic Bread W/ Olive Oil Dip | Gavi or Chardonnay | |
| Deviled Eggs | Rose Viognier | Rose |
| Bruschetta Pomodoro | Chianti, Light Pinot Noir | Rose of Malbec |
| Bruschetta Pesto | New Zealand Sauvignon Blanc | |
| Polish Sausage, Sliced In BBQ | Alsatian Gewurztraminer, Riesling or Tokay | |
| Crawfish Cajun Style | Pinot Grigio or Rose | |
| Chips and Salsa | Sangria | Rose' |
| Fried Shrimp | Riesling | |
| Queso Blanco | Fume Blanc | |
| Ribs | Old Vine Zinfandel | |
| Grilled Shrimp | Big, woody Chardonnay | |
| Shrimp, Clams, Oysters Fried With Tartar Sauce | Riesling German Kabinett | |
| Calamari Fried With Lemon | Decanted Prosecco | |
| Calamari Fried With | Chianti DOC or | Rose of Malbec |

| | | |
|---|---|---|
| Marinara Sauce | | |
| Caprese Salad | Veneto Pinot Grigio | Sauvignon Blanc |
| Prosciutto M/ Melon | Barolo, Merlot | Gattinara, Barbera |
| Roasted Asparagus | New Zealand Sauvignon Blanc | |
| Crostini With Bleu Cheese | Riesling | Gewurztraminer |
| Stuffed Mushrooms | Gamay, Beaujolais, Pinot Noir | |
| Baked Mini Crab Cakes | Unoaked Chardonnay | |
| Oven Fries | Oaked Chardonnay | |
| Pinwheels Turkey | Sauvignon Blanc | |

## Beef

| Food Selection | Wine | Alternative Wine Selection |
|---|---|---|
| Sirloin, Rare-Medium Rare | Cabernet Sauvignon, | Bordeaux, Meritage Blend, Malbec |
| Sirloin, Medium to Well Done | Big Merlot (Napa Sonoma) St.Emilion, Blends | |
| Steak Au Poive | Zinfandel | Petite Sirah |
| Rib eye Rare – Med-Rare | Australian, Napa Cabernet Sauvignon. | Meritage |
| Rib Eye Medium- Well Done | California Merlot | Old Vine Zinfandel |
| New York Strip Rare-Med-Rare | Cabernet Sauvignon, Bordeaux, | Meritage Blend, Malbec |
| New York Strip Medium - Well | Sonoma Merlot | Petite Sirah |
| Prime Rib Roast Center Cut Med Rare | Carneros Pinot Noir, | Napa Cabernet Sauvignon, Cabernet Sauvignon, Malbec |
| Prime Rib Roast End Cut Medium | Cabernet Sauvignon | Malbec |
| Filet Mignon Rare-Med-Rare | Cabernet Sauvignon, Carneros Pinot Noir | Cru Bordeaux, , Malbec, or French Burgundy, |
| Filet Mignon Medium-Well done | Meritage | Barolo Cabernet Sauvignon, Bordeaux |
| Tenderloin | Cabernet Sauvignon, Medoc | Pinot Noir |
| Chateaubriand | Bordeaux, Meritage Blend | Napa Cabernet Sauvignon |
| Rump Roast | Amarone, Cote Du Rhone, | Petite Sirah, Malbec |
| T Bone | Medoc Bordeaux ,Sonoma Cabernet Sauvignon, | Malbec |

| | | |
|---|---|---|
| Eye of Round Roast | Cabernet Franc, Merlot | Cabernet Sauvignon, |
| Skirt or Flank Steak | Shiraz, Zinfandel | Grenache |
| Steak Tartare | Pinot Noir, Crianza, Valpolicella | |
| All Blackened Beef | Old Vine Zinfandel, | Old Vine Garnacha |
| BBQ Brisket w/ Spicy BBQ Sauce | Old Vine Zinfandel | Zinfandel |
| Beef BBQ Ribs | Old Vine Zinfandel | Petite Sirah or |
| Deli Roast Beef | Australian Merlot, | Central Coast California Merlot |
| Beef Kabobs w/ veggies and steak seasoning | Shiraz, | Petite Sirah |
| Hamburger. | Merlot, Shiraz, | Cabernet Sauvignon or Rhone Blend, |
| Beef Wellington | Napa Cabernet Sauvignon, | Russian River Pinot Noir |
| Beef Bourguignon | Chateauneuf Du Pape / | Hermitage, Rhone blend |
| Beef Stroganoff | California Merlot | Malbec |
| Beef Stew | Merlot, Merlot Blend | Old Vine Zinfandel |
| Beef Stir Fry | , Shiraz | Petite Sirah |
| Beef Fajita | Shiraz | Petite Sirah |
| Meat Loaf | Merlot | |
| Meat Balls Italian | Merlot, | Nero D'Avola, Sangiovese |
| Beef Pot Pie | Pinot Noir, | Australian Style Merlot |
| Beef Hot Dogs | Beaujolais | Riesling, |

## Chicken

### *White Meat Breast*

| Food Selection | Wine | Alternative Wine Selection |
|---|---|---|
| Baked | Big, Woody Chardonnay | |
| BBQ Average (heat) | Old Vine Zinfandel | |
| BBQ medium Heat | Shiraz | Cote Du Rhone |
| BBQ very Spicy heat | Petite Sirah, | Rhone Blend |
| Panee' Sauté | Buttery Chardonnay | |
| Cordon Bleu | Buttery Chardonnay | Viognier |
| Parmesan | Chianti, | Sangiovese |
| Alfredo | Napa Style Chardonnay | Rose of Malbec |
| Marsala | Sonoma Pinot Noir | |
| Madeira | Rhone Blends | Cote du Rhone |
| Cacciatore | Chianti Classico, | Merlot |
| Piccata | New Zealand Sauvignon Blanc | |
| Teriyaki | Sonoma Zinfandel | |
| Lemon peppered | New Zealand Sauvignon Blanc | Decanted Prosecco |
| Pesto | New Zealand Sauvignon Blanc | Sancerre |
| Sweet and Sour | Old Vine Zinfandel | Petite Sirah |
| Fajitas | Un-Oaked Chardonnay | Dry Riesling |
| Salsa | Gewurztraminer | |
| Chicken Chili | Petite Sirah, Rhone Blend | Merlot |
| Ala King | Oaked Chardonnay | |
| Key West Chicken | Sauvignon Blanc | |
| Rosemary & Herb | Sauvignon Blanc | |
| Honey Mustard | Riesling | |
| Curried | Late Harvest Riesling, Spatlese | |

*All Chicken Parts*

| Food Selection | Wine | Alternative Selection |
|---|---|---|
| | | |
| Southern Fried | Crisp Riesling, Kabinett | |
| Cajun Battered | Late Harvest Riesling, Spatlese | |
| Honey Fried | Big, Rich Chardonnay | |
| Garlic Fried | Big, Rich Chardonnay | |
| BBQ sauce fried | Old Vine Zinfandel | |
| Whole Roasted Oven | Big, Buttery Chardonnay, | Rose of Pinot Noir |
| Spit/ Rotisserie | Big, Buttery Chardonnay, | Rose of Pinot Noir |
| Crock Pot slow cook | Pinot Noir | |
| Stew | Merlot, | |
| Fricassee | Viognier | |
| Enchiladas | Chardonnay | |
| Chicken Florentine | Sauvignon Blanc | |
| Stuffed | NZ Sauvignon Blanc | |
| Stroganoff | Big, Rich Chardonnay | |
| Traditional Chicken Soup | Big, Rich Chardonnay | |
| Italian Wedding Soup | Big, Rich Chardonnay | |
| Chicken and Dumplings | Big, Rich Chardonnay | |
| Chicken and Dumplings | Viognier, Rose of Malbec | |
| Chicken Pot Pie | Sauvignon Blanc | |

| | | |
|---|---|---|
| McDonald's, KFC, Wendy's | Riesling or Gewurztraminer | |
| Smoked | Rose of Pinot Noir, Nouveau Beaujolais | |
| Jamaican Jerk | Petite Sirah, Rhone Blend | |
| Hawaiian | Buttery Chardonnay | |
| Asian | Gewurztraminer | |
| Thai | Late Harvest Riesling, Spatlese | |
| Italian | NZ Sauvignon Blanc | |
| Sweet and spicy | Old Vine Zinfandel | |
| Sweet and Sour | Nouveau Beaujolais | Rose of Pinot Noir, |
| BBQ (medium sauce) | Zinfandel | |
| BBQ (spicy sauce) | Old Vine Zinfandel | |
| BBQ (very spicy hot) | Petite Sirah | |
| Lemon | Zinfandel | |
| Teriyaki | Petite Sirah, Rhone Blend | |
| Honey Sesame | Gewurztraminer | |
| Honey Citrus | Sauvignon Blanc, Viognier | |

## Pork

| Food Selection | Wine | Alternative Wine Selection |
|---|---|---|
| Chops Fried or Sautéed | Pinot Noir big, rich style | |
| Grilled No Marinade | Beaujolais AOC or Villages | Dry Rose Tavel |
| Baked Salt & Pepper | Viognier | Light style Pinot Noir |
| Crock Pot Slow Cooked | Merlot, | St. Emillion |
| Tenderloin Roasted Salt Pepper | Viognier | Light style Pinot Noir |
| Marinated Italian | Pinot Grigio | |
| Marinated Teriyaki | Old Vine Zinfandel, Petite Sirah | |
| Marinated Spicy BBQ sauce | Old Vine Zinfandel | |
| Marinated Lemon Based | Pinot Grigio | Decanted Prosecco or |
| **Pork Roast** Slow roast Heavy Herbal Crust | Big Woody Chardonnay | Fume Blanc |
| Slow roast Brown Gravy | Merlot, | Grenache |
| BBQ roast Charcoal slow roast | Old Vine Zin, | Rhone Blend |
| Pork pieces Crock Pot, slow cooked w/veggies | Merlot, | Rhone Blend |
| Slow cooked in and Italian Tomato Sauce | Barbera, | Nebbiolo |
| Pulled Pork BBQ Style Medium | Old Vine Zin | |
| Spicy, Hot | Petite Sirah | |
| Pork Spare Ribs W/ Sauerkraut | Riesling Spatlese | Late Harvest Riesling |
| Southern style | Merlot | Pinot Noir |
| Canadian Baby Back Ribs | Sonoma Zinfandel | Old Vine Zin |

| | | |
|---|---|---|
| Hot & Spicy Sauce | Petite Sirah, | Garnacha |
| BBQ w/ Medium Spice sauce | Rhone Blend, | Old Vine Grenache |
| **Ham** | | |
| Baked Brown Sugar Glaze | Pinot Noir | |
| Baked Polynesian, Hawaiian | Nouveau/ AOC Beaujolais | Light Pinot Noir |
| Honey Spiral cut | Nouveau/ AOC Beaujolais | Rose of Malbec |
| Fresh Ham Bone in | Nouveau/ AOC Beaujolais | Rose Of Pinot Noir |
| Ham Steak | Beaujolais, | Rose Of Pinot Noir |
| Ham and Bean Stew | Merlot | Cote Du Rhone |
| Bacon | Zinfandel | Primativo |
| **Sausage** | | |
| Italian Sweet Grilled | Zinfandel Cote Du Rhone | |
| Italian Hot Spicy Grilled | Petite Sirah | |
| Italian In Tomato Sauce | Petite Sirah Based Blend | |
| Andouille Creole | Petite Sirah, Shiraz | |
| Summer Sausage | Grenache, Tempranillo | |
| Andouille in Brown Roux Gumbo | Petite Sirah | |
| Oven roasted W/ accompanying Veggies | Rose of Pinot Noir | |
| Hawaiian style accompanying Veggies | Gewurztraminer | Rose of Pinot Noir |

## Veal

| Food Selection | Wine | Alternative Wine Selection |
|---|---|---|
| Sirloin Grilled or Broiled | Napa Cabernet, | Medoc, Bordeaux |
| Chop Fried, Broiled | Russian River Pinot Noir | |
| Shanks Braised | Malbec, | Northern CA Merlot |
| Cutlets | Pinot Noir | Petite Sirah |
| Ossa Bucca | Barolo, Gattinara, | Meritage Blend |
| Saltimbocca | Brunello Di Montalcino Dolcetto, | Rosso di Montalcino |
| Parmigiano | Chianti Classico, | Merlot |
| Scaloppini | New Zealand Sauvignon Blanc | Decanted Prosecco |
| Marsala | Nero D'Avola, | Merlot |
| Swiss Style | Buttery Chardonnay | |
| Hungarian Stew | Cote Du Rhone | Rhone Blend |
| Piccata/ Francese | Fume Blanc | Decanted Prosecco, |
| Weiner schnitzel | Riesling Spatlese | Gewurztraminer |
| Meat Balls | Merlot | Chianti Classico |
| Involtini | Chianti Classico, | Merlot |
| Oscar | Pinot Noir | Bardolino, Rose of Pinot Noir |

## Lamb

| Food Selection | Wine | Alternative Wine Selection |
|---|---|---|
| Chops Rare to Medium | Cabernet Sauvignon, Bordeaux | |
| Chops Well done | Merlot, | Petite Sirah |
| Leg Roasted, Heavily Seasoned crust | Cabernet Sauvignon, Bordeaux | Malbec |
| Leg Rosemary & Garlic | Cabernet Sauvignon, Bordeaux | Malbec |
| Shank Braised | Chateauneuf du Pape | Cote du Rhone |
| Stew Sloe Cooked | Cabernet Sauvignon, Bordeaux | Meritage Blend |
| Rack W/ Mint Pesto | Shiraz, Tempranillo | Crianza |
| Rack Crispy with Honey and Mascarpone Cheese | Petite Sirah, | Shiraz |
| Rack Grilled Marinated in Olive oil, Garlic and Lemon | Cabernet Sauvignon, Bordeaux | Malbec |
| Meat Balls Marinara | Merlot, Chianti Classico | Petite Sirah |
| Lamb Kabob BBQ Simple salt & pepper | Zinfandel | |

# Seafood

## *Crab*

| Food Selection | Wine | Alternative Wine Selection |
|---|---|---|
| Claws/ Mustard Sauce | Russian River Chardonnay, | Pouilly Fuisse |
| Crab cakes | Riesling, Kabinett | Gewurztraminer |
| Crab cakes Rémoulade Sauce | Primativo | Zinfandel |
| Crab cakes Ala Italiano | Chianti | |
| Tetrazzini | Viognier | , Unoaked chardonnay |
| Deviled | Rose of Malbec | |
| Omelet/ Frittata | Chardonnay | |
| Steamed | Buttery Chardonnay | |
| Newberg | Buttery Chardonnay | |
| Soft Shell | Gewurztraminer | |
| Stuffed | Chardonnay | |

## *Clams*

| Food Selection | Wine | Alternative Wine Selection |
|---|---|---|
| Raw on the half shell Cocktail / Horseradish sauce | Sonoma Sauvignon Blanc, | Champagne, Fume Blanc |
| Baked/ Stuffed | Big Woody Chardonnay | |
| Au Gratin | Big Woody Chardonnay | |
| Deep Fried Batter, Breaded | Riesling , Spatlese, Gewurztraminer | |
| Creole | Riesling , Spatlese, Gewurztraminer | |
| Steamers in Garlic | Chardonnay, | |

| | Russian River | |
| --- | --- | --- |
| White sauce w/ Linguini | Pouilly Fuisse, | Buttery Chardonnay |
| Red Sauce w/ Linguini | Pinot Noir | Chianti |
| Casino | Chardonnay, | |
| Chowder New England | Wooded, buttery Chardonnay | |
| Manhattan | Pinot Noir | |
| Clam Dip W/ Chips | Sauvignon Bland, New Zealand | |
| Stir-fried | Tempranillo | |

*Shrimp*

| Food Selection | Wine | Alternative Wine Selection |
| --- | --- | --- |
| Boiled | Buttery Chardonnay | Champagne |
| Grilled | Buttery Chardonnay | |
| Sautee' | Buttery Chardonnay | |
| BBQ K-Bobs | Buttery Chardonnay | |
| BBQ W Spicy Seasoning | Gewurztraminer | |
| Baked | Buttery Chardonnay | Decanted Prosecco |
| Broiled | Buttery Chardonnay | |
| Scampi | Buttery Chardonnay | |
| Newberg | Buttery Chardonnay | |
| Salad | New Zealand Sauvignon Blanc | Decanted Prosecco |
| Salad | Viognier | Prosecco |
| Breaded Fried | Riesling Kabinett | |
| Gumbo | Pinot Noir | |
| Shrimp Louis | Buttery Chardonnay | Champagne |
| Sweet & Sour | Sauvignon Blanc | Decanted Prosecco |
| Rémoulade | Gewurztraminer | |
| New Orleans Style | Riesling Spatlese | |
| Creole | Riesling Spatlese | |

| | | |
|---|---|---|
| Risotto | Buttery Chardonnay | |
| Etouffe | Rose of Pinot Noir | |
| Grilled | Riesling Spatlese | |
| Marinara | Chianti | |
| Florentine | Fume Blanc | |
| Blackened | Zinfandel, Garnacha | |

*Scallops*

| Food Selection | Wine | Alternative Wine Selection |
|---|---|---|
| Sautéed Butter & Garlic | Russian River Chardonnay | Pouilly Fuisse |
| BBQ Grilled | Chardonnay | |
| Blackened | Zinfandel | |
| In White wine sauce | Pouilly Fume | Fume Blanc, |
| Baked | Chardonnay | |
| Scampi w/Pasta | Pouilly Fuisse | Russian River Chardonnay |
| Broiled w/ Lemon | Decanted Prosecco | |
| Florentine | Sauvignon Blanc | Decanted Prosecco |
| Au Gratin | Chardonnay | |
| Fra Diavola | Petite Sirah, | Rhone Blend |
| Battered/ Fried | Gewurztraminer | Riesling |
| Tarragon Scallops | New Zealand Sauvignon Blanc | |
| Pernod Cream sauce | Pouilly Fuisse | Russian River Chardonnay |
| Herb/ Brown Butter | Sancerre | Fume Blanc, |
| Lemon Shallot | Prosecco | |
| Corn Chowder | Chardonnay, Unoaked | |
| Poached w/ Steamed Veggies | Russian River Chardonnay | Pouilly Fuisse |
| Marinara | Chianti | |

| | | |
|---|---|---|
| Etouffe | Petite Sirah, Rhone Blend | Rose of Pinot Noir |
| Cajun boil | German Riesling Spatlese | |

## Oysters

| Food Selection | Wine | Alternative Wine Selection |
|---|---|---|
| Raw Cocktail / Horseradish sauce | Champagne, Prosecco | |
| Stew | Viognier, Prosecco | |
| Rockefeller | New Zealand Sauvignon Blanc | |
| Bienville | New Zealand Sauvignon Blanc | |
| Grilled | Pinot Grigio | Fume Blanc |
| Soup | Chardonnay | |
| Fried | Gewurztraminer | |
| Casino | New Zealand Sauvignon Blanc | |
| Prosecco Bathed Oysters | Prosecco Decanted | |
| Po Boy | Riesling Kabinett | |
| Shooter | Buttery Chardonnay | |
| Stuffing | Chardonnay | |
| Gumbo | Pinot Noir | |
| Grilled | Riesling Spatlese | |

## Lobster

| Food Selection | Wine | Alternative Wine Selection |
|---|---|---|
| Steamed | Pouilly Fuisse, Meursault, | Carneros Chardonnay |
| Boiled | Pouilly Fuisse, Meursault, | Carneros Chardonnay |
| Broiled | Russian River | Pouilly Fuisse |

|  | Chardonnay |  |
|---|---|---|
| Baked | Pouilly Fuisse, Meursault, | Carneros Chardonnay |
| Tails in Champagne | French Champagne | Napa Sparkling wine |
| Fritters | Gewurztraminer |  |
| Stuffed | Chardonnay |  |
| Lobster Rolls | Sauvignon Bland, Viognier |  |
| Thermidor | Big Buttery Chardonnay |  |
| Chowder /corn | Big Buttery Chardonnay |  |
| Newberg | Chardonnay |  |
| Salad | New Zealand Sauvignon Blanc |  |
| Ceviche | New Zealand Sauvignon Blanc |  |
| Salad Nicoise | New Zealand Sauvignon Blanc |  |
| Gourmet Mac & Cheese | Carneros Chardonnay, Russian River Chardonnay |  |
| Pasta Marinara | Chianti DOCG |  |
| Fried | Riesling Kabinett |  |
| BBQ Grilled | Buttery Chardonnay |  |
| Ala King | Buttery Chardonnay |  |

*Fresh Fish*

| Food Selection | Wine | Alternative Wine Selection |
|---|---|---|
| **TUNA** | | |
| Tuna Albacore Baked, Broil | Viognier, Un-oaked Chardonnay | |
| Tuna Mahi Hawaiian | Gewurztraminer | |
| Tuna Mahi Grilled BBQ | Pinot Noir | |
| Tuna Ahi / Yellow fin Broiled | Big, Buttery Chardonnay | |
| Tuna Ahi / Yellow fin Blackened | Zinfandel | |
| Tuna Ahi / Yellow fin Sear Medium Rare | Pinot Noir | |
| Tuna Ahi / Yellow fin Balsamic Glaze' | Rose of Pinot Noir | |
| Tuna Ahi / Yellow fin Sesame crusted Ginger | Rose of Pinot Noir | |
| Tuna Ahi / Yellow fin Tomato Basil | Sauvignon Blanc | |
| Tuna Ahi / Yellow fin Carpaccio | Big, Buttery Chardonnay | |
| Tuna Ahi / Yellow fin Asian Sesame oils, Teriyaki | Gewurztraminer | |
| Tuna Ahi / Yellow fin Sushi, Sashimi | Gewurztraminer, Tepid Saki | |
| Tuna Ahi / Yellow fin Pan Fried Vinegar & Garlic | Prosecco Decanted | |
| **Catfish** | | |
| Fried, Corn Meal, Tartar Sauce | Gewurztraminer | |
| Fried, Batter hushpuppies, Tartar Sauce | Riesling, Washington State | |
| Coconut Catfish | Riesling, Washington St. | |
| Onion Crusted | Gewurztraminer | |

| | | |
|---|---|---|
| Blackened | chardonnay unoaked | |
| Sandwich w/ Chipotle dressing | Gewurztraminer | |
| Grilled , Tacos | Viognier, Fume Blanc | |
| Grilled Quesadillas | Pinot Grigio, Fume Blanc | |
| **COD** | | |
| Filet Baked | Buttery Chardonnay | |
| Broiled W/ Lemon Garnish | Viognier | |
| Sautéed | Chardonnay | |
| Deep Fried, Batter | Riesling Kabinett | |
| **Tilapia, White Fish, Red Snapper** | | |
| Baked, Broiled | Pouilly Fuisse, | Northern Cal Chardonnay |
| BBQ Grilled | Big Woody Chardonnay | |
| Blackened | Zinfandel | |
| Fried | Riesling Kabinett | |
| **Carp, Perch** | | |
| Baked Grilled, Broiled | California Chardonnay | Pouilly Fuisse |
| Blackened | Zinfandel | |
| W Lemon | Prosecco Decanted | New Zealand Sauvignon Blanc |
| **Trout** | | |
| Baked. Broiled, | Sancerre, Fume Blanc | |
| Pan Fried | Sauvignon Blanc | |
| BBQ Grilled | Sauvignon Blanc | |
| Salt Crusted | Chardonnay Unoaked | |
| W/ Lemon | Prosecco Decanted | |
| **Haddock, Marlin ,Bluefish, Shark, Halibut, Kingfish, Striped Bass** | | |

| | | |
|---|---|---|
| Baked. Broiled, | Pinot Grigio, Fume Blanc | |
| Pan Fried | Classic Sauvignon Blanc, | |
| BBQ Grilled | Classic Sauvignon Blanc | Rose of Pinot Noir |
| Herb Crusted | New Zealand Sauvignon Blanc | |
| W/ Lemon | Prosecco Decanted | |
| Blackened | Zinfandel | |
| **Orange Roughly, Mullet, Ling, Mullet, Sea Bass ,Flounder, Grouper, Snook** | | |
| Baked. Broiled, | Big, Woody Chardonnay | |
| Pan Fried | Fume Blanc, | Sancerre |
| BBQ Grilled | Chardonnay, Unoaked | |
| Herb Crusted | New Zealand Sauvignon Blanc | |
| W/ Lemon | Prosecco Decanted | New Zealand Sauvignon Blanc |
| Blackened | Zinfandel | Rose of Malbec , Anjou Rose |
| Nut crusted Pecans, Almonds, Cashews | Rose of Pinot Noir | |
| Cajun or Creole | Gewurztraminer or Riesling | |
| **Redfish, Amberjack, Sardine, Mackerel** | | |
| Baked. Broiled, | New Zealand Sauvignon Blanc, | Pinot Grigio |
| Pan Fried | Rose of Pinot Noir | |
| BBQ Grilled | New Zealand Sauvignon Blanc, | Viognier |
| Herb Crusted | New Zealand Sauvignon Blanc | |
| W/ Lemon | Fume Blanc | Prosecco |

| | | |
|---|---|---|
| Blackened | Zinfandel | |
| **Salmon, Sturgeon** | | |
| Grilled | Pinot Noir, | Sancerre, |
| Baked | Pinot Noir, | Big Buttery Chardonnay |
| Blackened | Zinfandel | |
| Sautéed, Pan Fried | Pinot Noir, Beaujolais | |
| Broiled | Pinot Noir, | |
| Cedar Plank | Zinfandel. Pinot Noir | |
| Poached   White wine & Water | Russian River Chardonnay | |
| Salad | Rose of Pinot Noir | |

## Italian

| Food Selection | Wine | Alternative Wine Selection |
|---|---|---|
| **Primo Piatti (Starters)** | | |
| Insalata Caprese | Pinot Grigio | Sauvignon Blanc |
| Antipasti Platter | New Zealand Sauvignon Blanc | Decanted Prosecco |
| Grilled Vegetable Salad | Pinot Grigio | Fume Blanc, |
| Roasted Squash and Beef Carpaccio Salad | Dolcetto. | Pinot Noir |
| Risotto Croquettes: Arancini Di Riso | Sauvignon Blanc | |
| Bruschetta Pesto | New Zealand Sauvignon Blanc | |
| Bruschetta with Sautéed Mushrooms | Barbera D'Asti, Pinot Noir | |
| Bruschetta Pizzaiola | Chianti DOCG | |
| Margherita Pizza | Pinot Grigio | |
| Pesto Pizza | Sauvignon Blanc, Gavi | |
| Fiori Di Zucchini: Fried Zucchini Flowers | Riesling, | |
| Tuscan Bread Salad | Gavi, Chardonnay | |
| Involtini Di Carpaccio: Rolled Beef Carpaccio | Dolcetto, | |
| Sausage and Stracchino Cheese Crostini | Chianti Classico. Nero D'Avola | |
| Tender Artichoke Hearts | Decanted Prosecco | New Zealand Sauvignon Blanc |
| Pinzimonio: Vinaigrette | Prosecco Decanted | |
| **Zuppa (Soup)** | | |

| | | |
|---|---|---|
| Zuppa di Porcini: Porcini Soup | Pinot Noir | |
| Zuppa di Vongole: Clam Soup | Chardonnay, Gavi | |
| Cannellini and Pancetta Soup | Pinot Noir, Chianti DOCG | |
| Pasta E Fagioli Tuscan Bean Soup | Pinot Noir Rosso Di Montalcino. | Chianti Classico |
| Pasta with Prosciutto and Lettuce | Sangiovese, Nero d'Avola | |
| Conghilie with Clams and Mussels | Big Buttery Chardonnay | |
| **Pasta** | | |
| Lasagna | Merlot, | Barbera d'Asti |
| Manicotti | Merlot, | Barbera d'Asti |
| Gnocchi Red Sauce | Dolcetto, | Merlot, Nero D'Avola |
| Stuffed Shells | Merlot, | Barbera d'Asti |
| Vodka Pasta | Pinot Noir, | Chianti DOCG |
| Fettuccine Alfredo | Chardonnay, | Gavi, Pinot Grigio |
| Fettuccine con Carciofi: Fettuccine with Artichokes | New Zealand Sauvignon Blanc | |
| Pappa Al Pomodoro | Fume Blanc, | Pinot Grigio |
| Beet Risotto with Truffle Oil | Brunello, Rosso D'Montalcino | |
| Pasta with Beans and Mussels | Pinot Noir | |
| Lemon-Basil Orzotto | Prosecco Decanted | |
| Pesto Lasagna | Sauvignon Blanc | , Friuli Pinot Grigio |
| Spaghetti with Bay Scallops, Guanciale and Parsley | Big, Buttery Chardonnay | |
| Zesty Spaghetti a la Puntenesca | Zinfandel, Dolcetto d'Alba | |
| Red Sauce and Spaghetti | Merlot Chianti Classico | |
| Pasta with Butter | Big Chardonnay | |

|  |  |  |
|---|---|---|
| and Cheese |  |  |
| Drunken Spaghetti | Pinot Noir, |  |
| Tagliolini con Tartufo: Tagliolini with Truffles | Rose of Pinot Noir |  |
| Spaghetti Alla Caprese | New Zealand Sauvignon Blanc |  |
| Fettuccine with Squash and Parmesan-Lemon Cream Sauce | Prosecco, Decanter or not |  |
| Gorgonzola and Porcini Mushroom Risotto | Merlot, Barolo |  |
| Salsicce Con Cima Di Rapa: Sausage with Broccoli Rabe | Chianti Classico, Amarone |  |
| Spinach Stuffed Braciole in a Sunday Sauce with Pappardelle | Valpolicella |  |
| **Entrée** |  |  |
| Osso Buco | Brunello Di Montalcino |  |
| Swordfish with Puntenesca Sauce | Sauvignon Blanc |  |
| Mussels, garlic & Wine Sauce | Big, woody Chardonnay |  |
| Staccato al Chianti: Beef Braised in Chianti | Rosso D' Montalcino, | Tuscan Petite Sirah, Chianti Classico Riserva |
| Spezzatino di Cinghiale: Wild Boar Stew | Barbaresco, | Barolo, Petite Sirah |
| Meatballs with a White Wine Sauce | Pinot Noir, Bardolino |  |
| Beef Tenderloins con Balsamic | Petite Sirah |  |

| | | |
|---|---|---|
| Grilled Tuscan Chicken | Chianti Classico, Valpolicella | |
| Lumache di Mare: Sautéed Sea Snails | Chardonnay, Big and Buttery | |
| Baccala Alla Pizzaiola: Cod with Tomato | Bardolino | Rose of Pinot Noir, |
| Braciole with Gravy | Chianti Riserva, Nero. D'Avola | |
| Chicken Scaloppini with Sage and Fontina Cheese | Russian River Chardonnay | |
| **Dolci (Dessert)** | | |
| Crostata with Raspberry Jam | Rose of Pinot Noir | |
| Tiramisu | Brachetto D'Aqui | |
| Lemon Ricotta Cookies with Lemon Glaze | Prosecco | |
| Espresso Chocolate Mousse with Orange Mascarpone Whipped Cream | Amarone, | Recioto della Valpolicella |
| Chocolate Sformato with Amaretto Whip Cream | Amarone, | Recioto della Valpolicella |
| Castagnaccio: Chestnut Flour Cake | Amarone | , Recioto della Valpolicella |
| Panna Cotta al Mango | | Moscato D' Asti |
| Soufflé Al Cioccolato | Amarone, | Recioto della Valpolicella |
| Biscotti Di Prato | | Moscato D' Asti |
| Risotto Al Cioccolator: Chocolate Risotto | Amarone, Recioto della Valpolicella | |
| Strawberries with | Brachetto D'Aqui | |

| | | |
|---|---|---|
| Balsamic Vinegar | | |
| Hazelnut Crunch Cake with Mascarpone and Chocolate | Asti DOCG | |
| Ricotta with Vanilla-Sugar Croutons and Berries | Moscato D' Asti | |
| Cannoli | Moscato D' Asti | |
| Rum Baba | Moscato D' Asti | |
| Sfoidelle | Moscato D' Asti | |
| Neapolitans | Moscato D' Asti | |

# Oriental

| Food Selection | Wine | Alternative Wine Selection |
|---|---|---|
| **Appetizers** | | |
| Egg Rolls Soy, Duck Sauce | Gewurztraminer | |
| Spring Rolls Soy, Duck Sauce | Gewurztraminer | |
| Crab Rangoon Soy, Duck Sauce | Riesling ,WA State, | |
| Sushi   Soy, ginger, Wasabi | Riesling, WA State, | |
| Sashimi  Soy, ginger, Wasabi | Riesling, Kabinett | |
| Dim Sum | Gewurztraminer | |
| Pork Spare Ribs | Old Vine Zinfandel | |
| Pu Pu Platter | Old Vine Zinfandel | |
| Sesame Chicken wings | Gewurztraminer | |
| Shrimp Toast | Gewurztraminer | |
| Beef Teriyaki Skewers | Zinfandel, Petite Sirah | |
| **Soup** | | |
| Won Ton | Big Woody Chardonnay | |
| Egg Drop | Sonoma Sauvignon Blanc | , Muscadet or Fume Blanc |
| Hot & Spicy | Rose of Pinot Noir | |
| Sizzling Rice | Gewurztraminer | |
| Miso | Sauvignon Blanc | |
| **Shrimp** | | |
| Sweet and Sour | Rose of Pinot Noir | |
| W/ Lobster Sauce | Big, Woody Chardonnay | |
| Garlic Shrimp | Gewurztraminer | |
| Cashew Shrimp | Gewurztraminer | |

| | | |
|---|---|---|
| Honey Walnut | Gewurztraminer | |
| Pineapple | Rose of Pinot Noir | |
| Szechwan | Gewurztraminer | |
| **Beef** | | |
| W/ Broccoli | Merlot | |
| W/ Stringed Beans | Petite Sirah | |
| Garlic | Merlot | |
| Moo Shu | Pinot Noir | |
| Mongolian | Merlot | |
| Hunan Spicy | Petite Sirah, | Cote Du Rhone |
| Szechwan | Petite Sirah, | Cote Du Rhone |
| Chow Mein | Pinot Noir | |
| Chop Suey | Pinot Noir | |
| Lo Mein | Merlot | |
| Oyster Sauce | Cabernet Sauvignon | |
| Beef in Black Bean Sauce | Cabernet Sauvignon | |
| Pepper Steak | Zinfandel | |
| Ginger Beef | Petite Sirah, Cote Du Rhone | |
| Beef with Broccoli Stir-fry | Merlot | |
| Beef with Spicy Black Beans | Old Vine Zinfandel | |
| Beef with String Beans | Old Vine Zinfandel | |
| Beef with Three Vegetables | Pinot Noir | |
| Beef with Tomatoes | Merlot | |
| Chinese Clay-Pot Beef | Meritage, Petite Sirah Blend | |
| Honey | Zinfandel | |
| Hibachi Japanese | Cabernet Sauvignon, Merlot | |

## Oriental Thai

| Food Selection | Wine | Alternative Wine Selection |
|---|---|---|
| Thai Chicken Breast | Alsace Gewurztraminer | |
| Sesame Noodles | Chenin Blanc, Riesling | |
| Thai Turkey | Alsace Gewurztraminer | |
| Coconut Rice | Sauvignon Blanc | |
| Noodles in Peanut Sauce | Alsace Gewurztraminer | |
| Shrimp & Spinach Curry | Alsace Gewurztraminer | |
| Butternut Squash Soup | Pinot Noir | |
| Thai Basil Vegetables | New Zealand Sauvignon Blanc | |
| Thai Shrimp | Alsace Gewurztraminer | |
| Thai Cucumber Salad | New Zealand Sauvignon Blanc | |
| Thai Pumpkin Soup | Pinot Noir, Beaujolais | |
| Thai Beef | Shiraz or Petite Sirah | |
| Thai Burgers | Shiraz or Petite Sirah | |

## Authentic Spanish

| Food Selection | Wine | Alternative Wine Selection |
|---|---|---|
| Spanish Colette(Tortilla de patatas) | Chardonnay, Albarino | |
| Caldereta, Fish Stew | Sauvignon Blanc, Albarino | |
| Gazpacho | Tempranillo | |
| Paella Seafood | Big, Woody Chardonnay | |
| Paella Saffron | Sauvignon Blanc, Albarino | |
| Chicken and Seafood Paella | Sauvignon Blanc, Albarino | |
| Chicken in Garlic Sauce | Chardonnay, Albarino | |
| Fresh Tuna Fish | Albarino | |
| Oxtail Stew | Rioja Crianza or Reserva | |
| Cochinillo Asado Roasted Suckling Pig | Tempranillo, Shiraz | |
| Pulpo a la Gallega (Galician Octopus) | Gewurztraminer | |
| Gambas Ajillo (Garlic Prawns) | Gewurztraminer | |
| Jamon Iberico and Chorizo (Iberian Ham And Spicy Sausage) | Gewurztraminer | |
| Pescado Frito (Fried Fish) | Gewurztraminer | |
| Queso Manchego | Tempranillo, Garnacha | |
| Patatas Bravas (Fried Potatoes in Spicy Sauce) | Petite Sirah, Pinotage | |

## Mexican/Tex-Mex

| Food Selection | Wine | Alternative Wine Selection |
|---|---|---|
| **Enchiladas** | | |
| Chicken or cheese filled | Chardonnay | |
| Beef or Pork filled | Tempranillo or Shiraz | |
| **Nachos** | | |
| Cheese/ Jalapenos | Pinot Grigio, Dry Riesling | |
| Beef and Cheese | Beaujolais | |
| **Beef** | | |
| Carne asada, grilled beef | Merlot, Shiraz | |
| Carne guisada, stewed beef | Cote du Rhone, Petite Sirah blend | |
| Chicharrón and Chicharrone | Chardonnay | |
| Chilaquiles | Chardonnay | |
| Chile relleno | Gewurztr4aminer | |
| Chimichangas (Tex-Mex mostly) | Big, Woody Chardonnay | |
| Chorizo | Shiraz | |
| Empanadas | Tempranillo or Shiraz | |
| Beef Fajitas | Tempranillo or Shiraz | |
| Chicken Fajitas | Viognier, Gewurztraminer | |
| Shrimp Fajitas | Big, Woody Chardonnay | |
| Flautas | Beaujolais, , Pinot Noir | |
| Gorditas | Sauvignon Blanc, | |

| | | |
|---|---|---|
| Memela | Shiraz | |
| Pollo Encacahuatado | Chardonnay | |
| Pollo motuleños | New Zealand Sauvignon Blanc | |
| Pollo picado | New Zealand Sauvignon Blanc | |
| Pollo rostizado | New Zealand Sauvignon Blanc | |
| Quesadillas | Gewurztr4aminer | |
| Salbutes | Gewurztr4aminer | |
| Sopes | Gewurztr4aminer | |
| Sopa de tortilla (tortilla soup) | New Zealand Sauvignon Blanc | |
| Sonoran hot dog | Tempranillo or Shiraz | |
| Tacos | Tempranillo or Shiraz | |
| Tamales | Tempranillo or Shiraz | |
| Taquitos | Tempranillo or Shiraz | |
| Tostadas | Tempranillo or Shiraz | |

# Greek

| Food Selection | Wine | Alternative Wine Selection |
|---|---|---|
| Moussaka Egg Plant Casserole | Petite Sirah | |
| Tiropites | Chardonnay Unoaked | |
| Chicken Soup Avgolemono | Chardonnay Buttery | |
| Pastitsio | Merlot, | |
| Galaktoboureko - | Moscato d'Asti | |
| Fassolatha | Pinot Noir, , | Cote Du Rhone |
| Spanakopita | New Zealand Sauvignon Blanc | |
| Baklava | Asti, Moscato | |
| Youvetsi | Cabernet Sauvignon, | Malbec |
| Dolmathakia | Retsina , | New Zealand Sauvignon Blanc |
| Fassolakia Lathera | Shiraz | |
| Pork Souvlaki | Merlot, Shiraz | |
| Domates Yemistes | Meritage Blend, Cote du Rhone | |
| Keftethes | Merlot | |
| Kourabiethes | Moscato d'Asti | |
| Feta Greek Salad | Sauvignon Blanc, Pinot Grigio, | Gavi d' Gavi |
| Spanakorizo | decanted Prosecco | |

## Cheese

| Food Selection | Wine | Alternative Wine Selection |
|---|---|---|
| All Blue Veined cheese, | Port, Moscato D'Asti | Riesling Auslese |
| Swiss, Jarlsberg, Ementhaler | Most White Wines | Pinot Noir and Beaujolais |
| Most Cheddars | Zinfandel, Shiraz | Cabernet Sauvignon |
| Brie, Camembert, Goat cheese | Pinot Noir, Cote Du Rhone, | Oaky Chardonnay |
| Mahon, Manchego | Tempranillo, Shiraz, Grenache | Merlot |
| Bel Paese, Port Salute, | Sauvignon Blanc, | Pinot Grigio, Gavi d' Gavi |
| Super sharp Cheddar, Beechers, | Chianti Classico, | Merlot, Shiraz, Barolo |
| Boursin, herbal infused cheeses | New Zealand Sauvignon Blanc | Prosecco |
| Monterey Jack, Gouda, Havarti | Merlot, | Chardonnay, Pinot Gris, Pinot Grigio |
| Mascarpone, Flavored Ricotta | Moscato, Asti Spumante | Decanted Prosecco |
| Gourmandise | Moscato, Asti Spumante | Decanted Prosecco |
| Parmigiano, Asiago | Barolo, Cabernet Sauvignon, | Grenache Chianti Classico |

## Venison

| Food Selection | Wine | Alternative Wine Selection |
|---|---|---|
| Chili | Old Vine Zinfandel | |
| Stew | Cote du Rhone, | Petite Sirah |
| Braised | Cabernet Sauvignon, | Amarone |
| Grilled | Petite Sirah, l | Zinfandel |
| Meatloaf | Merlot | |
| Chicken Fried w/Gravy | Shiraz | Merlot |
| Slow cooked W/Veggies | Cabernet, Sauvignon, Meritage | |
| BBQ Spicy BBQ Sauce | Old Vine Zinfandel | |
| Fried Marinated in Worcestershire sauce & Garlic | Petite Sirah, Zinfandel | |
| Burgers | Merlot | |

*Eating is a necessity. Dining is an Experience.*

# Chapter 6
# Glossary of Terms

**Acerbic** - Sharp, Bitter-like,

**Acidic** - Tart, Biting

**Balance** - Between Acid and Fruit (can be found in the Bouquet, Mouth Feel and the Finish)

**Bouquet** - Aroma. Nose feel, Smell

**Carbonic Maceration** - "Whole Berry Fermentation" After Harvest, the uncrushed grapes placed in a sealed Fermentation vat; then filled with Carbon Dioxide gas. The $CO_2$ will permeate the skins and start fermentation inside the grape, producing a short-lived fruity wine with a high acid content.

**Fat** - Lacking acid; overly full feeling in the mouth

**Hints** - Usually felt in the finish or the breathing out through the nose. Scents are brought forth by offering the Olfactory Receptors a second time while exhaling through the nose

**Jammy** - This is a richness (or Viscosity) felt in the fullness of the mouth.

Juicy- This is another mouthfeel, bringing the fruit flavors, well forward in the taste

**Legs** - Usually has to do with the level of alcohol in the wine and the speed at which it evaporates, thicker and slower legs can indicate a higher alcohol level.

**Malolactic** - Usually best in Chardonnay, The sharp Malo acids are transformed into the rich Lactic acids giving the wine a bigger, fuller bodied feel

**Mouth Feel** - The mouth can only detect sweetness, bitterness, cold and heat  Acids and sparkle will give the inside of the mouth

**Nose** - Bouquet, aroma, smell

**Oily** - big rich mouth-filling wine with an almost sticky feel on the palate. Found often when wines are served too warm

**Sharp** - Biting or bitterness in the mouth

**Soft** - Round, rich flavors that have subtle tannins and acids
**Spicy** - Sassy, blend of zesty flavors and mouth-feel

**Tannin** - tannin is a textural element that makes wine taste dry.  Important to the aging of red wines

**Velvety** - The texture or feel in the mouth and passing through the esophagus, Velvety wines flow very smoothly

**Woody** - Wine that has been fermented and, or aged in wood barrels. The wood flavors are transferred into the wine

## *Epilogue*

There are actually thousands of grape varieties growing in every feasible condition and vineyard location throughout the globe. It's obvious that we can't possibly discuss every wine regarding food or not. So, I have tried to select wines and foods that are readily available to the American market. Further, in our guide section, I have selected over 600 different dishes with matching wines. Clearly, we cannot list all dishes and their variations. So we have compiled what I believe is the most complete list of food that would be available to consumers in the American market. We have also taken the matching to a different level by offering a second or possibly a third selection based on your local availability. I hope you enjoy the attached apps and will utilize them to enhance your dining pleasure. From time to time we will be amending the apps to include new dishes and suggestions from you. Bon Appetite!

Made in the USA
San Bernardino, CA
31 October 2015